Directionscore:
Selected and New Poems

DIRECTIONSCORE:

Selected
and New Poems

Don L. Lee

bp

BROADSIDE PRESS
12651 Old Mill Place   Detroit, Michigan 48238

First Edition
First Printing, February 1971

Copyright © 1967, 1968, 1969, 1970, 1971
by Don L. Lee

LCN: 76-142060
ISBN: Paper 0-910296-48-0
ISBN: Cloth 0-910296-49-0
ISBN: Special Edition 0-910296-50-2

Back cover photograph by KATUARA PETERS
Manufactured in the United States of America

A DEDICATION

The totality of this work, that which is positive, was influenced in part by:

blackmusic and its musicians who are too numerous to mention

the positive work of the Nation of Islam under the practical and spiritual guidance of the Honorable Elijah Muhammad

Africa and African people everywhere; we are beginning to love each other, to learn to move together as a people.

CONTENTS

"I've heard liberal-minded Frenchmen express genuine horror at the lynching of a Negro by Mississippi whites. But to an Asian or an African it was not a Mississippi white man who did the lynching; it was a Western white man. It is difficult for white Western Europe to realize how tiny Europe is in the minds of most people of the earth. Europe is indeed one world, small, compact, white, apart. . . ."

—*Richard Wright*

Renaissance I
to Renaissance III ?:
An Introduction

Hoyt Fuller, the perceptive editor of *Black World* (formerly *Negro Digest*) calls today's movement in the black arts "the New Black Renaissance." His title implies that there was a renaissance before this one; he also suggests that today's work in the arts has some relationship to the first. If so, how? Is the present movement a duplication of the first? And why a "New Black Renaissance" now?

John A. Williams has said that

The Renaissance flowered because Black Artists were exotic and the great wonder was that they could perform in their individual arts at all, being Black. Great dependence was placed on whites already in the arts for entrance into the American arts community.

Let us note that last sentence again, "Great dependence was placed on whites already in the arts for entrance into the American arts community." Mr. Williams goes on to say

By and large, Renaissance artists, once they were recognized to any small degree, at once became middle-class, removed to a large extent from the masses, although many of them, having no where else to go, returned to the masses for material.

Brother Williams also notes that the major difference between the first renaissance and today's renaissance is that today's renaissance is political, whereas the first was not.

Harold Cruse in the *Crisis of the Negro Intellectual* also alludes to many of the same weaknesses in renaissance I. In essence, Mr. Cruse doesn't doubt that works of art were produced during the twenties. What he and the younger black writers of today question is 'What good did the work do?' By and large, who reads Langston Hughes, Jean Toomer, Claude McKay, Wallace Thurman and the others? What are the positive effects that the first black renaissance had on the masses of black people who lived and worked during that period? In his first autobiography, *The Big Sea,* Langston Hughes himself admitted,

> I was there. I had a swell time while it lasted. But I thought it wouldn't last long . . . For how could a large and enthusiastic number of people be crazy about Negroes forever? They thought the race problem had at last been solved through Art plus Gladys Bentley . . . I don't know what made many Negroes think that—except that they were mostly intellectuals doing the thinking. The ordinary Negroes hadn't heard of the Negro Renaissance. And if they had, it hadn't raised their wages any.

My answer to this question is that the black arts movement in the twenties was of a minimal influence and virtually went unnoticed by the majority of black people in the country. More whites knew about what was happening than brothers and sisters. One of the main reasons for the short life of renaissance I is that no black people, other than the artists themselves, were involved in it. No lasting institutions were established. The musicians, even though they created the only indigenous music, produced few if any of their own records and didn't birth one living recording company. With all the writers and poets that flowered during that period, they didn't establish one mass producing publishing company, and most, if not all, of the published works that we read today are undoubtedly controlled by European-

Americans. Roughly the period of the "Harlem Renaissance" was between 1917 and 1930.

Essentially what we are saying is that the movement today is about survival. The major difference between the twenties and the seventies is that among the black artists of today there is no such thing as being apolitical. To be apolitical, when our very lives are influenced and controlled by political power, is to be extremely foolish. It is either not to care or to be in agreement with those who wish to systematically force us from this earth.

Now, what I'm saying is that black people do what we are *supposed* to do. In essence, we do what we've been *taught* to do. We are products of European-American culture and therefore there are certain things expected of us and to deviate is to be radical, like—letting your hair grow long, or not wearing a tie, etc. We're also products of the Christian-Judeo ethic and we are taught from infancy to be very aggressive and competitive. (However, that competition and aggressiveness are generally directed toward each other and not toward the real enemy.) That means at every level we compete with each other, consciously and unconsciously. We as *educated people* are more confused because we're supposed to be able to think for ourselves—and we do, *sometimes.*

Many of us knowingly and purposefully misinterpret today's youth and others who advocate an ideology that's not strictly pro-U.S.A., or pro-European-American, pro-Western. My people, do you realize that in terms of what power is in this country and the world, we have none. We have no power at all. Black people in this country don't manufacture anything nationally except hair spray and rhetoric. We don't distribute anything nationally except fear and mis-information, and we have the audacity to talk about green power, black capitalism and other lightweight things. One wonders if the proponents of black capitalism really understand what capital is, what economy is?

In terms of acquiring any *real* wealth or power in this country, the odds are so great against blacks that most of the economic prognosticators don't believe that it will ever happen unless blacks will be able to change their color. Just from a light reading of G. William Dormoff's *Who Rules America and The Higher Circles,* C. Wright Mills' *The Power Elite,* Kenneth Lamott's *The Money Makers* or Ferdinand Lundberg's mammoth study *The Rich and the Super-Rich* we can begin to understand the powerlessness of blacks. In Lundberg's study we're only mentioned in terms of being used politically (e.g. Democrats in Chicago), in terms of being systematically overlooked by the monied/private clubs, as when he says

> It is doubtful if any Negro has ever been so much as proposed for membership. It would be erroneous to say Negroes are barred. They simply are not noticed. Negroes fall under the latter-day integrationist rule: They are not discriminated against as Negroes but it so happens they are found to be unqualified because of a tragic history over which the latter-day keepers of the keys have no retroactive control. The point is only: They couldn't get accepted even if they could fly to the moon and back in a kite.

> Beyond this, as far as the clubs are concerned, Negroes not only lack titles to property (as quite a few Jews do not) but no one of them seems to be within 250 years of ever having them in any significant proportions. Who would a Negro be likely to inherit from?

With the wave of black consciousness, we have in many areas the opening up of "black" banks. Whereas one can argue their usefulness, Andrew F. Brimmer, a governor of the Federal Reserve System, dismissed them in a recent speech at a Detroit convention when he labeled black banks "as ornaments rather than vital instruments of economic development." He also inferred that the black banks' major investments were not in the black community, but in white areas.

The new voices are not talking about tearing up, but building, about nation building—Imamu Baraka says "It's Nation Time." You see the main difference between renaissance II and renaissance I is that the people are involved. And they are about change and survival and building. The present day institutions are in some cases beyond any meaningful change and if you can't change the institutions, most likely you'll be changed. For instance, when we read that the Institute of the Black World had severed its relationship with the Martin Luther King Memorial Center, one automatically put the blame on the Institute, rather than question the real reasons behind the break-up. Do you realize that when any institution or group tries to benefit black people here and elsewhere, there seems to be projected by the mass media that somehow the participants are incompetent and/or racists. Yet, these are some of the same people you and I worked with less than three years ago, and you mean that all of a sudden they've lost their competence, and have stooped to the non-productive area of klanism. But here is a better example of building and powerlessness.

In November of 1970 the territorial boundaries of the nation of Guinea were violated by Portuguese invaders. However, the mass media picked the holocaust up and treated it like somebody had stepped on an ant. Think, black people, think! Whenever anything happens in Europe or in the Middle East (which is Africa—but distorted also by the

15

media controllers), we get a *full report* and sometimes a *special*. But Africa and especially those parts of Africa ruled by independent men is of no consequence. *Unless* there is a coup d'etat, and then we read nothing but smiles *disguised* as *objective* reportage. So all we had to go on about Guinea was conflicting news coverage that asserted that the cause may have been due to *internal dissension*. What steps do big Negroes take now—or do they care? Will there be a seven thousand dollar ad in the Sunday *New York Times* telling this country to send arms and men to Guinea, as was done for Israel (occupied Palestine.)

We were insulted last year when the Honorable Julius Nyerere visited this country for the twenty-fifth anniversary of the United Nations and was snubbed by the President of this country. Yet, when Golda Meir visited this country, you would have thought it was a national holiday. Here she is head of an illegal country of less than three million, being received like royalty, and Brother Nyerere, the head of a country of thirty-five million black people or more, being virtually ignored by the officials of this country. The Honorable Kenneth Kaunda of Zambias' visit went virtually unnoticed by the officials of this country. Yet, can you imagine any head of state from Europe coming here and not being received like royalty? The State Department in the ultimate insult left the ambassadorship to Kenya open for seven months, which is unthinkable in any European country. But then again, it's our fault. I said we have no power. The Jew that we out-number almost six to one has more power than we have. And I submit that one of the reasons for this is that we have not developed a national consciousness among our people.

Renaissance I failed to do the job. Nobody doubts that those who took part in that movement didn't leave us a foundation to grow on; that's not the problem. Renaissance II exists in part because of brothers like W. E. B. DuBois, Charles S. Johnson, Claude McKay, Jean Toomer, James Weldon Johnson, Marcus Garvey and others. The problem is that they produced no on-going, life-giving or life-saving institutions. Another problem that is still with us is we are the only people who happen to be something other than what we are. We're the people who happen to be black. It's always a writer who happens to be "negro," a doctor who happens to be "negro," an athlete who happens to be "negro." Yet, there are no W.A.S.P. writers who happen to be W.A.S.P.'s or Jewish scientists who happen to be Jews. No. We are black people first and products of our vocation second. We are black people who happen to be doctors, lawyers, writers, etc.

PAN-AFRICANISM AND FOREIGN POLICY:

The word "Pan" means all, every or the entirety. Pan plus African, to put it simply, means one Africa or African people moving toward one-ness. Yes, we black people in this country and the world are an African people. This is not to romanticize Africa. We understand that Africans in terms of peoples, language, customs, religions, habits and other things that rule people's daily lives are just as diverse as Europeans are. However, we didn't become Negroes until around 1620. Before that we were Africans or black men and women. Every other people in this country came from land with a name to it. After careful study, many intuitive, well researched and informative papers and much time and money, we finally realize that there is no such place as Negro-land. It seems that we're the only people without roots, if we continuously accept others' definitions of ourselves. We're an African people whose experiences for the most

17

part have been controlled, directed and nurtured by European-American culture. Brother Stokely Carmichael in his perceptive essay "Pan-Africanism, The Highest Stage of Black Power" in the the fall of 1970 issue of *Rhythm Magazine* relates to us his concept of the settler colony which is well worth repeating.

> I want to talk now about settler colonies. A settler colony is created when the European leaves Europe, comes to an area, takes over the land, and dominates the traditional owners of the land. My wife is from South Africa. South Africa is a settler colony. Rhodesia (which is really named Zimbabwe) is a settler colony. Europeans leave Europe, go to Zimbabwe, change its name to Rhodesia, and call themselves Rhodesians. Angolo is a settler colony. Guinea Bissau is a settler colony. Australia is a settler colony . . . Israel is a settler colony. European Jews leave Europe, go to Palestine, change the name to Israel and dominate the land.

> But, . . . more importantly for you and for me, we must come to understand that America and Canada are settler colonies. This is difficult for us to accept because they are close to being successful settler colonies. In order to be a successful settler, one must commit genocide against the traditional owners of the land, and that is exactly what the Europeans have done. After committing genocide, they changed the name to America. They called themselves Americans. When you call them Americans, you make it sound as if they belong here. You do that because you want to call yourselves Black Americans and you want to feel that you also belong here. But if we analyze history, and if we agree that revolutions are based on historical analysis, we will see that they are not

Americans. They are in fact, European settlers. That's all they are. Now I know what you will say. You will say, "Oh, but that happened a long time ago." It might have happened five thousand years ago, but I am talking about history and what is fact.

If they are European settlers, guess what we are? We can't be no Afro-Europeans or Black Europeans. We have to be an African people. See, if we say we are Americans, Black Americans, or Afro-Americans, it means that we participated in committing genocide against the red man. Since we did not, there's no need for us to call ourselves black Americans.

Carmichael believes that the highest form of black power is Pan-Africanism. He, as does the white boy, knows that when you are talking about power and nation-building, you have to talk about land. Black people control no land to mention in the U.S.A., and remember, brothers and sisters, *land is the only thing that nobody is making any more of;* we can buy those bell bottoms next year, or that 225, but land is going action fast and that white boy is hip to it, for he, all over the world, is taking it—action fast. And he's not doing it with love—because if love was power, we would rule the world. Africa is important because it is *us,* and it is about land.

Brother Carmichael believes that that land base can be Africa. He says,

Our ideology must be Pan-Africanism, because we said that in a revolution one must have a land base. Now where best can black people in this country get a land base? This is where the difficulty will arise. Many people will say that we can get a land base in America. Well, if we know anything about capitalism in America, we

19

know that the white boys not going to give up *no land*. You got to take every inch of the ground from him.

The revolutionary formula for taking land is simply to seize, to hold and to develop. That's how we are going to have to take land in the country. But I say that if we could seize the land, we wouldn't be able to hold it; and if we could hold it, we wouldn't be able to develop it.

Brother Carmichael is realistic and practical enough to realize that blacks from this country are not going to pack up and go *back* to Africa, especially since most of us have never been there in the first place. But what he and others are trying to do is open up other possibilities to us, to give us other alternatives, and to force us to seriously question our existence in this country.

For black people in this country to consider the importance of foreign policy in relation to Africa *is* foreign. When black people read the daily paper, we are not expected to get anything of substance, *and we don't.* Most of us, when we read the paper, the first thing we read is the sports page or the gossip column. We don't know what an editorial page is and those of us that do sometimes take the contents lightly, passing it off with "This dosen't concern us." Everything this white boy does concerns us. No matter how remote it may seem. In 1967, when the *Report From Iron Mountain* was printed, many blacks brushed it aside thinking that it was about iron ore in some mountain. Only very recently have we begun to develop a serious group of black people who impart knowledge without fear.

Remember, Pan-Africanism is concerned about survival, concerned about developing a sophistication for survival. It's not an easy job; the white boy has had think tanks for about twenty years and we are definitely playing catch up.

NATIONALISM:

When we talk about black nationalism, we are just starting from the basics. As Maulana Ron Karenga says, our ultimate reality is that we're black. No one calls a Jewish nationalist a racist; a W.A.S.P. nationalist is not considered anti-nothin'! It all gets down to who has the power to define. We don't. So other people put on us their definitions. Nationalism means that people stick together and move together in the best interests of themselves. We've been white nationalists. White nationalism has been (and still is) our philosophy and it is very difficult to see the contradictions because we've been white nationalists since birth. We are certainly not Marxists or capitalists, but niggers don't mind calling themselves anything that's a part of Europe. But when we define ourselves, we continuously run into trouble. Nationalism simply says that we must have control over the space which we occupy. That means that any and everything which has some effect upon our daily lives we must have some say so over, if not the ultimate say-so. Nationalism means moving to control the police departments, catholic churches, public schools, any and everything that functions in our community. It means the development of an effective Public Relations system; it means publishing our own books and pressing our own records; it means taking AM radio and making it functional and educational, rather than just entertaining (put Imamu Baraka in between James Brown and Aretha Franklin; put DuBois and Julius Nyerere between Joe Tex and Diana Ross, etc.) Nationalism is serious movement toward controlling the controllable.

BLACK STUDIES AND BLACK EDUCATION:

Black Studies is not a synonym for Pork Chop Studies. It's not about teaching people what soul food is, as Bayard Rustin would have us believe. When we talk about a Studies Program, we mean to study that part of us as African people which has enabled us to endure, to study in substance what will advance us as a people. We understand as do Africans from the continent that in order to deal with the technological world, one needs technology. That's real! Some of the African nations still send their sons and daughters to the West to study, even with the fear that their sons' and daughters' minds may be co-opted by capitalism, Marxism, hippyism, and mini-skirtism. Yet, they, as we, understand that this is not a game to make a few people rich and popular. We're talking about developing areas of discipline which will encourage and ensure survival and growth. Nobody questions Jewish studies, or European studies, or Japanese studies, or Chinese studies, and we can go on. Only when black people decide to deal with themselves do others try to deal with us. We're about defining and legitimizing our own existence; directing our own course in space; recognizing our own priorities. Black Studies is not a restriction; it's a commitment. It's not a reaction, but an act. We can study any area of the life forces that affect us. We need to study white people, to try to understand why they are so anti-good and pro-evil. We must move beyond pettiness of nothingness. Why should we be threatened by each other? All that says is that we're insecure and un-sure of our own worth.

As I said earlier in this essay, African people do what *we are supposed* to do; we do what we have been *taught* to do. The Honorable Elijah Muhammad has said that if a people continuously send the children to the enemy to be educated, no doubt about it, the children will mirror their teachers. The children's values and aspirations will become the same as those of his teachers. We need not question the validity of his argument—all we have to do is just critically and unemotionally look at ourselves. Why are we so divided; so small and petty in many of the things that we do; so un-positive about ourselves and unsure about that which we *can* do. Obviously we've been taught to be that way.

Black education will deal with black people, give us tools that are necessary for positive development in any area. Black education is anti-anything that tends to limit us mentally and physically. For instance, if we had the right type of education, hazards such as drugs would not be a problem. We wouldn't have brothers and sisters taking trips and copping out and becoming hippies. They would know that the abundance of drugs in our community is a subtle system of control. The brothers and sisters would know that outsiders control and encourage the flood of drugs in our community. Mario Puzo in his book, *The Godfathers* relates it this way:

In my city I would try to keep the traffic in the dark people, the colored. They are the best customers, the least troublesome and they are animals anyway. They have no respect for their wives or their families or for themselves . . .

The Negroes were considered of absolutely no account, of no force whatsoever. That they had allowed society to grind them into the dust proved them of no account and his mentioning them in any way proved that the Don of Detroit had a mind that always wavered toward irrelevancies.

The important thing about quoting Puzo is that he in his

novel considers black people as animals, but even more startling is that the Don of Detroit had the audacity to even mention the blacks in the context of drugs. Puzo says the Don "had a mind that always wavered toward irrelevancies." Do you understand this? He is saying that drugs among blacks are taken for granted and to even bring it up is to waste time and deal in irrelevancies." That's a hell of a statement about a people. We had better wake up, because if we haven't peeped ourselves, you can be sure that others have peeped us and all the drug programs, all the commercials against them, or all the preaching to the young is about as effective as a no-smoking sign on a Chicago subway.

In closing I say, if you are not upset and concerned about today's events, then perhaps, just perhaps, you don't know what's happening. You see, we understand that the white boy works three shifts a day; we work one for *him;* on the second shift we talk about what others are not doing and should be doing; and on the third, we get high and sleep for four hours, wake up and go to work and wonder why we're behind. The worldrunners are serious about maintaining control. If we as black people, as African people, do not move together to do the *possible,* to do what is necessary in this the "New Black Renaissance" or renaissance II, I doubt if any of us or our people will be around to read the poetry of renaissance III. We say organize wherever you are, the schools, the churches, the prisons; but first the walls of your own mind. Don't think about getting others together if you don't *know the way* yourself. Be what you teach. Learn from others. The white boy was the first to organize on color and he's on top. Don't get caught up in defending your blackness—you are not racist and if you were you would have been taught to be. Move into righteousness. Quote Nyerere and Toure like you quote Lenin and Marx. Put Africa on the brothers' minds. Work toward a nation like the Jehovah Witnesses sell *Watchtower* and *Awake*. Build as well as you think you love, lover, and the 1980's will be for humans.

—don l. lee
January, 1971

Think Black

1965-1967

*I learned what manhood was by
observing what manhood was not.*

CONTENTS

Think Black

1965-1967

*I learned what manhood was by
observing what manhood was not.*

This book is dedicated to all Black People—where ever
you are.

d. l. l.

ERRATA

Page 104, line 2 should read "like" for "life."
Page 111, line 2 should read "black" for "back."

Continuation from page 105
"A Poem to Complement Other Poems"

know the realenemy. change. know the realenemy. change
    yr/enemy change know the real
change know the realenemy change, change, know the
    realenemy, the realenemy, the real
realenemy change your the enemies/change your change
    your change your enemy change
your enemy. know the realenemy, the world's enemy.
    know them know them know them the
realenemy   change your enemy   change your change
    change change your enemy change change
change change your change change change.
your
mind nigger.

CONTENTS

INTRODUCTION

I was born in slavery in Feb. of 1942. In the spring of that same year 110,000 persons of Japanese descent were placed in protective custody by the white people of the United States. Two out of every three of these were American citizens by birth; the other third were aliens forbidden by law to be citizens. No charges had been filed against these people nor had any hearing been held. The removal of these people was on racial or ancestral grounds only. World War II, the war against racism; yet no Germans or other enemy agents were placed in protective custody. There should have been Japanese writers directing their writings toward Japanese audiences.

Black. Poet. Black poet am I. This should leave little doubt in the minds of anyone as to which is first. Black art is created from black forces that live within the body. These forces can be lost at any time as in the case of Louis Lomax, Frank Yerby and Ralph Ellison. Direct and meaningful contact with black people will act as energizers for the black forces. Black art will elevate and enlighten our people and lead them toward an awareness of self, i.e., their blackness. It will show them mirrors. Beautiful symbols. And will aid in the destruction of anything nasty and detrimental to our advancement as a people. Black art is a reciprocal art. The black writer learns from his people and because of his insight and "know how" he is able to give back his knowledge to the people in a manner in which they can identify, learn and gain some type of mental satisfaction, e.g., rage or happiness. We must destroy Faulkner, dick, jane and other perpetuators of evil. It's time for DuBois, Nat Turner and Kwame Nkruma. As Frantz Fanon points out: destroy the culture and you destroy the people. This must not happen.

Black artists are culture stablizers; bringing back old values, and introducing new ones. Black art will talk to the people and with the will of the people stop the impending "protective custody."

America calling,
negroes.
can you dance?
play foot/baseball?
nanny?
cook?
needed now. negroes
who can entertain
ONLY.
others not
wanted.
(& are considered extremely dangerous.)

d. l. l.

Back Again Home
(confessions of an ex-executive)

Pains of insecurity surround me;
    shined shoes,
    conservative suits,
    button down shirts with silk ties,
    bi-weekly payroll.

Ostracized, but not knowing why;
    executive haircut,
    clean shaved,
    "yes" instead of "yeah" and "no" instead of "naw,"
    hours, nine to five. (after five he's alone)

"Doing an excellent job, keep it up;"
    promotion made—semi-monthly payroll,
    very quiet—never talks,
    budget balanced—saved the company money,
    quality work—production tops.
    He looks sick. (but there is a smile in his eyes)

He resigned, we wonder why;
    let his hair grow—a mustache too,
    out of a job—broke and hungry,
    friends are coming back—bring food,
    not quiet now—trying to speak,
    what did he say?

    "Back Again,

        BLACK AGAIN,

            Home."

"Stereo"

I can clear a beach or swimming pool without
        touching water.
I can make a lunch counter become deserted
        in less than an hour.
I can make property value drop by being seen
        in a realtor's tower.
I ALONE can make the word of God have little
        or no meaning to many
        in Sunday morning's prayer hour.
I have Power,
BLACK POWER.

You Finish It
(I loved, I love)

>   Let us talk the two of us,
>   about silly things like ivory tusks
>   and books
>   and busts.
>
>   When we tire we'll start again
>   communicating about fins and pins
>   and insects
>   and gin.
>
>   We'll talk throughout the day
>   and steal a smile along the way,
>   we'll cuss and fuss
>   and
>   love with lust.
>
>   We'll exist with bills and pills
>   and
>   intellectual thrills
>
>   We'll catch each others eye—Blush—make
>   an excuse or two and then we'll smile
>   and laugh
>   and fight
>   and cry.

33

A Poem for Black Women

    i mean
    i
    thought she was
    it.

    "blackmen ain't shit,"
    she would say.
    &
    the words would
    cut thru me
    like rat
    teeth
    forced thoughts
    would
    think, "i'll try harder."

    i mean
    she was strong
    & beautiful
    & had a natural
    that
    was layen there.
    & her built in
    words
    hurt so much,
    too much:
                "blackmen ain't shit,"

& me,
  "i'll try harder."

i mean
that woman moved
me.
  (i even hit on her a couple of times)
&
dreamed about
our union
two black people groovin &c., &c.
un
til
  i saw her
on the other side
natural & all,
smiling those words:
     "blackmen ain't shit,"
& holding that whi
te boy's
hand.

Understanding but Not Forgetting
(for the Non-Colored of the World)

I drank Dubonnet and began to meditate—
out loud.

About my brother, he reads the NEW YORK TIMES,
WASHINGTON POST and attends HOWARD
    UNIVERSITY
and still ain't hip.

About his girl friend and her coming out party,
if she was ready—she would be trying to stay
IN.

About my grandmother who may have finished the
third grade—she is the wisest person I know.
Behind all those ain'ts, us'ens and we's lies
a mind with wisdom that most philosophers would
envy.

About my history professor who literally reads
his lectures (lies) from the text and places a
mandatory class attendance on us.
About the week ends at home when everybody was
drunk and I got all the money I wanted—no family
but money.

About the homosexual who slapped his boy friend—
his boy friend began to bleed. It seems as
though the homosexual had razor blades between
his fingers.

About me, as I seek the truth, wondering if my
mind is not getting all fucked up—or am I
learning something?

About my sister with five children before the
age of 22, she has never known a day of happiness
or is it I who have never known a day of happiness?

About positive images as a child—NONE.

About my mother whom I didn't understand—but
she read Richard Wright and Chester Himes and
I thought they were bad books.

About my blackness and my early escape
period, trying to be white.

About the nights my mother would go out—
without money—to get us something to eat,
she always came back with food. Some people
would call this prostitution but I call it—
providing for her family.

About the NUN who came to the Chicago Slums
for a summer and discovered Negroes—I mean
they were people too. She is back now,
as a lay christian, in the SLUMS . . . teaching . . .
. . . "us niggers."

About the white station master cheating me on
the returns from my paper route and telling
me what a good boy I was and "keep up the
good work" and me SMILING. I needed the job.

About the woman whom I often talked to and
loved. She went to college and then she bought
a wig—I still know her but she doesn't know
me.

About the strength I gained from living in the
slums. I was mentally deficient but physically

strong—I had to be.............to live.

About negative images as a child—all black.

About the Catholic Church, which I sought out, it failed drastically.

About the rent, lights and gas parties at 25 cents a head.

About the American Ideal—DEMOCRACY—and how I used to believe in it.

About the "Protestant Ethic" and "Social Darwinism," more excuses to crush you with— if you are black.

About the labor unions, they use you on the picket lines and keep you in a line after the strike.

About psychology—you are still inferior with technical terms and pretty diagrams.

About black history—non-existent.

About death, an alcoholic's death, MOTHERS

About eating habits, anything I could get.

About Christ, he was white too.

About reading—with my mouth, not my mind.

About the BLACK MIDDLE CLASS, the white ones.

About civil rights, I mean "niggers" rights.

About Malcolm X, he started people to thinking— BLACK.

About the peripatetic preacher and his never
ending calls—at the wrong time.

About the "Culturally Deprived"—another way
to say niggers.

About the American System—will it change
before it's too late—AND BEFORE I AND OTHERS
STOP GIVING A DAMN.

Wake-up Niggers
(you ain't part Indian)

                    were
                    don eagle & gorgeous george
                    sisters
                    or did they just
                                act that way—
                    in the ring,
                    in alleys,
                    in bedrooms of the future.
                                (continuing to take yr/money)
                    have you ever
                    heard tonto say:
                                "i'm part negro?"
                                    (in yr/ mama's dreams)
                    the only time
                    tonto was hip
                    was when he said:
                                "what you mean WE,
                                    gettum up scout"
                    & left
                    that mask man
                    burning on a stake
                                crying for satchel paige
                    to throw his
                    balls
                    back.

&
you followed him niggers—
all of you—
            yes you did,
                    i saw ya.
on yr/tip toes
with
roller skates
on yr/knees
            following Him
down the road,
                not up
following Him
that whi
te man with
that
cross on his back.

Re-act for Action
(for brother H. Rap Brown)

re-act to animals:
                    cage them in zoos.
re-act to inhumanism:
                    make them human.
re-act to nigger toms:
                    with spiritual acts of love & forgiveness
                    or with real acts of force
re-act to yr/self:
                    or are u too busy tryen to be cool
                    like tony curtis & twiggy?
re-act to whi-te actors:
                    understand their actions;
                    faggot actions & actions against yr/dreams
re-act to yr/brothers & sisters:
                    love.
re-act to whi-te actions:
                    with real acts of blk/action.
                    BAM BAM BAM

42

re-act to act against actors
who act out pig-actions against
your acts & actions that keep
you re-acting against their act & actions
stop.
act in a way that will cause them
to act the way you want them to act
in accordance with yr/acts & actions:

                           human acts for human beings

re-act
NOW niggers
& you won't have to
act
false-actions
at
your/children's graves.

Quiet Ignorant Happiness

My thoughts wander among the
Wombs of virginal women.
I do not necessarily desire them.
There is a sense of newness and immaculacy,
That cannot be found elsewhere
In this wretched word.

Her black thighs, smooth and untouched
                             and unblemished
By the constitution, its preamble and
The bill of rights need not concentrate on
Existing.
That warm entrance to beauty which someday
May open up and seek the "promised land"
Will forever be envied by me.

The viridity that babies lose,
Once released,
Will remain within her.
There is no vision there—she need
Not be blinded by deceptions and obliquities.
The untouched will dwell free and happy
                           and OPTIMISTIC

I dread the day when
Her womb is broken,
For then
        she will ask for . . .

EQUALITY.

In a Period of Growth

       like,
       if he had da called me
       black seven years ago,
       i wd've—
              broke his right eye out,
              jumped into his chest,
              talked about his momma,
              lied on his sister
              & dared him to say it again
       all in one breath—
       seven years ago.

Awareness

BLACK	PEOPLE	THINK
PEOPLE	BLACK	PEOPLE
THINK	PEOPLE	THINK
BLACK	PEOPLE	THINK—
THINK	BLACK.	

Black Pride

1967-1968

You can't love or give
love
if you can't be found

I would like to dedicate this book to brothers
Malcolm X,
Langston Hughes
and
John Coltrane
All innovators in their own way.

INTRODUCTION

In James Gould Cozzens' novel *By Love Possessed,* there is a Negro sexton who "came last to the altar rail . . . by delaying, he took care that members of the congregation need never hesitate to receive the blood of Our Lord Jesus Christ because a cup from which a Negro had drunk contained it." In other words, the sexton accepted his white fellow Christians' notion of himself as unclean, and acted accordingly. It is this acceptance of white America's values which degrade black people that causes black school children to cringe when they hear the words "black" or "Africa." Young Chicago poet Don L. Lee combats this tendency in his second book, *Black Pride.*

Part of the book is confessional, where the poet records his own hang-ups:

> I remember the time
> when I could
> smile—
> smiles of
> ignorance

and the hang-ups of his people:

> raped our minds with:
> T.V. & straight hair,
> Reader's Digest & bleaching creams,
> tarzan & jungle jim,
> used cars & used homes

He satirizes the black revolutionist who talks black and sleeps white, the traitorous preacher, and white power:

> with power to define, whi
> te power; indians were never
> the victors—they massacred

In "The Wall," he celebrates Chicago's mural where
    black artists paint,
> dubois/garvey/gwen brooks
> stokely/rap/james brown
> trane/miracles/ray charles
> baldwin/killens/muhammad ali
> alcindor/blackness/revolution

our heroes, we pick them for the wall
the mighty black wall

But it is not his recital of received pieties which makes
him a poet. Don Lee is a poet because of his resourcefulness
with language. He writes for the man in the street, and uses
the language of the street, and sometimes of the gutter, with
wit, inventiveness, and surprise. He assimilates into poetry
the words of a sign by Chicago mayor Richard J. Daley,
joins words together or splits syllables into fractions for
greater expressiveness. His shorter lyrics have a sting and his
longer poems a force that make him one of the most inter-
esting of the revolutionary young black poets.

In this second, *Black Pride,* there is a distinct advance
in poetic skill over his first book, *Think Black,* which we
can observe with pleasure and which indicates that we can
look forward to his rapid growth.

Detroit
October 1967

—Dudley Randall

50

The New Integrationist

> i
> seek
> integration
> of
> negroes
> with
> black
> people.

The Cure All

> The summer is
> coming.
> CONGRESS HAS ACTED:
> money into the
> ghetto,
> to keep the weather
> cool.

Two Poems
(from "Sketches from a Black-Nappy-Headed Poet")

last week
my mother died/
& the most often asked question
at the funeral;
was not of her death
or of her life before death
                              but
why was i present
with/out
a
tie on.

i ain't seen no poems stop a .38,
i ain't seen no stanzas brake a honkie's head,
i ain't seen no metaphors stop a tank,
i ain't seen no words kill
& if the word was mightier than the sword
pushkin wouldn't be fertilizing russian soil/
& until my similes can protect me from a night stick
i guess i'll keep my razor
& buy me some more bullets.

On the Discovery
of Beautiful Black Women

This metamorphic game seemed
      never to end—
though not a game,
     for games are played,
              played at, into, around and
are enjoyed.
My game is you—
          my game ceased to be enjoyed,
          then
I realized that it was not a game,
          but something called—
Life,
    and it sparkled,
              sparkled,
                 sparkled like a
Jewelsparkled—

         when I looked.

The Self-Hatred of Don L. Lee
(9/22/63)

i,
at one time,
loved
my
color—
it
opened sMALL
doors of
tokenism
&
acceptance.
      (doors called, "the only one" & "our negro")
after painfully
struggling
thru Du Bois,
Rogers, Locke
Wright & others,
my blindness
was vanquished
by pitchblack
paragraphs of
"us, we, me, i"
awareness.

i
began
to love
only a
part of
me—

my inner
self which
is all
black—
&
developed a
vehement
hatred of
my light
brown
outer.

The Only One

i work days, (9 to 5)
in the front office
of a well known Chicago
company.
this company is,
"an Equal Opportunity Employer,"
you can look at Me
and tell—everybody does.
my job??
it's unclear, it's new,
created just for me,
last week.
(after a visit from some human righters)
i've been with the company
for 15 years—
at last they gave me my own desk,
(toilet, lunch area & speeches too)
they like me—
(i mind my own business)
i've had, two years of college.
(it didn't matter until now)
They
call me an
EXECUTIVE—
but we,
you and i,
know the
Truth.

In the Interest
of Black Salvation

Whom can I confess to?
The Catholics have some cat
They call father,

　　　　　　　　mine cutout a long time ago—
Like His did.
I tried confessing to my girl,
But she is not fast enough—except on hair styles,

　　　　　　　　　　　　clothes
　　　　　　　　　　　　face care and
　　　　　　　　　　　　television.
If ABC, CBS, and NBC were to become educational stations
She would probably lose her cool,

　　　　　　　　　　　and learn to read

Comic Books.
My neighbor, 36-19-35 volunteered to listen but
I couldn't talk—
Her numbers kept getting in the way,
Choking me.
To a Buddhist friend I went,
Listened, he didn't—
Advise, he did,

　　　　"pray, pray, pray and keep one eye open"
I didn't pray—kept both eyes open.

Visited three comrades at Fort Hood,
There are no Cassandra çries here,
No one would hear you anyway. They didn't.
Three tried to speak, "don't want to make war."

　　　　　　　　　　　　　　why??

When you could do countless other things like
Make life, this would be—
Useless too . . .

When I was 17
I didn't have time to dream,
Dreams didn't exist—
Prayers did, as dreams.
I am now 17 & 8,
I still don't dream.
Father forgive us for we know what we do.
Jesus saves, '
          Jesus saves,
                    Jesus saves—S & H Green Stamps.

The Black Christ

without a doubt
rome did the whi
te thing when it
killed

           christ

it has been proven
that j. c. was non-whi
te in the darkest
way possible

           black ink on whi
           te paper

contradictions
from the west
ern cowBoys

           with two guns & music
           written on paper with
           black lines

it makes mary in-
to a first class
whore
john the bas
tard on
ly got people
wet
the cat
holic church cried
all the way to the
bank

           most of the priests
           are still in the
           ghettos—pimping

                              left the pope in
                              a soup line on st.
                              paul's day sold his
                              gold filled teeth
                              to a smiling jew
                              riding on a black
                              jackass

moses was hanged
in effigy by
smiling negroes
tearing up the
first commandment
judas became the
hero of the west
ern world & nick
named it lady bird

                    she got it from
                    a cat named parker

                                        she ain't been
                                        right sense

all the negro
preachers are driv
ing volkswagens & back
in night high school

                        taking black speech
                        & black history

off one god
can't get hooked
on another elijah

                    negro & whi
                    te cops riding
                    each other in
                    dark ghettos

negro cops with
naturals & whi
te minded negroes
with naturals wigs

                        more whi
                        te people read
                        ing fanon than
                        blacks

they know
all in sun try
ing to get black

                        man tan ain't
                        gone to get it
                        you can't hide
                        tomorrow is here

history repeats
itself   ask
st. malcolm
all because j. c.
was a nigger

                        the only things
                        that didn't change
                        were his
                        words

the world's best
seller
had sold out

                        (to bible reading eskimos.)

The Primitive

taken from the
shores of Mother Africa.
the savages they thought
we were—
they being the real savages.
to save us. (from what?)
our happiness, our love, each other?
their bible for
our land. (introduction to economics)
christianized us.
raped our minds with:
T.V. & straight hair,
Reader's Digest & bleaching creams,
tarzan & jungle jim,
used cars & used homes,
reefers & napalm,
european history & promises.
Those alien concepts
of whit-teness,
the being of what
is not.
against our nature,
this weapon called
civilization—
they brought us here—
to drive us mad.
(like them)

The negro
(a pure product of americanism)

     Swinging, Swinging,
               thru cotton fields,
               small southern towns,
               big ghetto darkness where
               his mind was blown,
     Swinging, Swinging,
               to assimilation into whi
               te madness called civilization/
               by those whc have the
               power to define,
     Swinging, Swinging,
               with power to define, whi
               te power; indians were never
               the victors—they massacred/
               black history was booker t.
               & george c. & a whi-te lie
               over black truth,

Swinging, Swinging,

        with ray charles singing
        the star spangle banner/
        all his soul didn't change the
        colors/red, white & light blue,

Swinging, Swinging,

        working, saving all year/
        working, saving to buy
        christmas gifts for children/
        just to tell them a whi
        te santa claus brought them.

Swinging, Swinging,

        into aberration where there
        is a black light trying to
        penetrate that whi-teness
        called mr. clean,

Swinging, Swinging,

        into blackness/away from
        negroness/to Self to
        awareness of basic color/
        my color, i found it,

Swinging, Swinging,

        by

            his

                neck. (nigger)

The Wall
(43rd & Langley, Chicago, Ill.
painted by the artists and
photographers of OBAC 8/67)

sending their negro
toms into the ghetto
at all hours of the day
(disguised as black people)
to dig
the wall, (the weapon)
the mighty black wall (we chase them out—kill if necessary)

whi-te people can't stand
the wall,
killed their eyes, (they cry)
black beauty hurts them—
they thought black beauty was a horse—
stupid muthafuckas, they run from
the mighty black wall

brothers & sisters screaming,
"picasso ain't got shit on us.
send him back to art school"
we got black artists
who paint black art
the mighty black wall

negroes from south shore &
hyde park coming to check out
a black creation
black art, of the people,
for the people,

art for people's sake
black people
the mighty black wall

black photographers
who take black pictures
can you dig,
                blackburn
                le roi,
                muslim sisters,
                        black on gray it's hip
they deal, black photographers deal blackness for
the mighty black wall

black artists paint,
                du bois/garvey/gwen brooks
                stokley/rap/james brown
                trane/miracles/ray charles
                baldwin/killens/muhammad ali
                alcindor/blackness/revolution
our heroes, we pick them, for the wall
the mighty black wall/about our business, blackness
                                can you dig?
if you can't you ain't black/   some other color
negro maybe??

the wall,
the mighty black wall,
"ain't the muthafucka layen there?"

Contradiction in Essence

i
met
a
part
time
re
vo
lu
tion
ist
too—
day

(natural hair, african dressed,
always angry, in a hurry &c.)

talk
ing
black
&
sleep
ing
whi
te.

A Poem for Black Minds

first. the color black/naturally
beautiful canNOT be mixed with whi
teness . . . . must not
it's
mine. ours throughout black nights
with guns watching . . . . . them.
we fucking/naturally.   non-proper
without thoughts of evil or insecure
feelings. me. we. living. they existing.
love can be a reality/thru blackness
& other colors dark. watch negroes. whi
te minds. enemies of black people. blew
their minds literally with whi
te thought & images of western whi
te woman. denying self. some see.
trying to come back
to us.
ain't you glad you is/black?
me too.

69

The Death Dance
(for Maxine)

my enemy steps mashed
your face in a mad
rhythm of happiness.
as if i was just learning to
boo-ga-loo.

my mother took the
'b' train to the loop
to seek work & was laughed at by
some dumb, eye-less image maker as
she scored idiot on "your" i. Q. test.

i watched mom;
an ebony mind
on a yellow frame.
"i got work son, go back to school."
(she was placed according to her
intelligence into some honkie's kitchen)

i thought & my steps
took on a hip be-bop beat
on your little brain
trying to reach any of
your senseless senses.

mom woul come home late
at night & talk sadtalk
or funny sadtalk. she talked
about a pipe smoking sissy
who talked sissy-talk & had
sissy sons who were forever playing
sissy games with themselves

70

& then she would say,
"son you is a man, a black man."

i was now tapdancing on your
balls & you felt no pain.
my steps were beating a staccato
message that told of the past 400 years.

the next day mom cried &
sadtalked me. she talked about
the eggs of maggot colored,
gaunt creatures from europe
who came here/put on pants, stopped eating with their hands
stole land, massacred indians,
hid from the sun, enslaved blacks &
thought that they were substitutes
for goods. she talked about a
faggot who grabbed her ass as
she tried to get out of the
backdoor of his kitchen & she said,
"son you is a man, a black man."

the African ballet
was now my guide; a teacher of self &
the dance of a people.
a dance of concept & essence.
i grew.

mom stayed home & the
ADC became my father/ in projects without
backdoors/"old grand dad" over
the cries of bessie smith/
until pains didn't pain anymore.

i began to dance dangerous steps,

warrior's steps.
my steps took on a cadence with other blk/brothers
& you could hear the cracking of
gun shots in them & we said that,
"we were men, black men."

i took the 'b' train to the loop &
you SEE me coming,
you don't like it,
you can't hide &
you can't stop me.
you will not laugh this time.
you know,
that when i dance again
it will be the
Death Dance.

The Traitor

he wore
a whi
te
shirt
&
bow tie,
a pretty
smile
&
the people called him
doctor.
(honorary degrees from fisk,
tenn. state a&i, morehouse &c.)

KA BOMMMM
KA BOMMMM

blood
splattered
his whi
te
shirt
his face
dis-
figured
by shot

gun
pellets
&
his head
fell
against
his
black
cadillac
&
bent
his
"clergy"
sign
toward the
black earth
&
somebody said,
"deal baby . . . . deal."

No More Marching

didn't i tell you
it would do no good

but you done gone
to school & read
all them books

now you is marchen
& singen
"we shall overcome"
getten hit &
looken dumb/&
smilen

holden that whi
te girls hand pro
tecten her

that makes you
equal too??
wheres your mom?
whos protecten her?
            (protect the motherhood
            not mother?)
is you a fool
fool
i guess you done
got what you wanted
            (setting next to her
            on a toilet continuing
            to eat whi-te shit)
my leaders? is you
mad
lead you to get

mo papers signed

world war 2
110,000 japs in
concentration camps
in home of slaves land of few

world war 3
ussr, england, france & u ass
                    vs.
third world
30 million niggers in
uncle's concentration camps
                (formerly called public
                housing)

in whi-te a
mer i cause they
knew

you better wake up
wake up
before it's

too late

killed
marchen in gage
park chicago
ill

caught brick in
head while tryen
to protect whi
te

girl.

Don't Cry Scream

1968-1969

a scream can be silent
pick your own time & place
and part your lips softly

Dedication/myself is them/u

first: to all blackmothers & especially mine (maxine) who will never read this book but said to me in my early years:
                    nigger, if u is goin ta open
                 yr/mouth *Don't Cry, Scream.*
which also means: *Don't Beg, Take.*
& second, which is really first: to the realpeople, us; blackpeople.

gwendolyn brooks   hoyt w fuller   dudley randall   ameer baraka   marvin x   david llorens   k william kgositsile barbara ann teer   jewel latimore   walter bradford   james cunningham   carolyn m rodgers   etheridge knight   margaret t g burroughs   rochelle ricks   marion graves   h rap brown   ebon   curtis   ellis   regina drake   ronda davis randson c boykin   freda high   my oldman where-ever he is omar lama   art mcfallan   onetha   eugene perkins   chester givens   jill witherspoon   sonia sanchez   pat smith joe goncalves   s e anderson   norman jordan   ahmed legraham alhamisi   sterling plumpp   earnestine   dondi lee askia muhammad toure   jackie   pew wee   blood   larry neal   all the brothers in prison   butch   nikki giovanni mary jane   pharaoh sanders   a b spellman   francis & val ward   ruwa chiri   lessie mims   david diop   ted joans gerald mcworter   stephen henderson   mari evans   sarah webster fabio   john o killens   margaret walker   catherine bobb hamilton   margaret danner   alicia l johnson   betty curtis   my black students at cornell   to those of u whose names do not appear above   thisisu thisisu thisisu go ahead, anyhow.

in the name of Allah, the Beneficent, the Merciful.

As-Salaam-Alaikum,
d l l

78

A FURTHER PIONEER
By Gwendolyn Brooks

At the hub of the new wordway is Don Lee.

Around a black audience he puts warm healing arms.

He knows that the black man today must ride full face into the whirlwind—with small regard for "correctness," with limited concern for the possibilities of "error." He knows that there are briefs even for the Big Mistake. The Big Mistake is at least a violent Change—and in the center of a violent Change are the seeds of creation.

Don Lee knows that nothing human is elegant. He is not interested in modes of writing that aspire to elegance. He is well-acquainted with "elegant" literature (what hasn't he read?) but, while certainly respecting the advantages and influence of good workmanship, he is *not* interested in supplying the needs of the English Department at Harvard and Oxford nor the editors of *Partisan Review,* although he could mightily serve as fact factory for these. He speaks to blacks hungry for what they themselves refer to as *"real* poetry." These blacks find themselves and the stuff of their existence in his healthy, lithe, lusty reaches of free verse. The last thing these people crave is elegance. It is very hard to enchant, with elegant song, the ears of a fellow whose stomach is growling. He can't hear you. The more interesting noise is too loud.

Don Lee has no patience with black writers who do not direct their blackness toward black audiences. He keeps interesting facts alive in his mind. "I was born into slavery in Feb. of 1942. In the spring of that same year 110,000 persons of Japanese descent were placed in protective custody by the white people of the United States. . . . No charges had been filed against these people nor had any hearing been held. The removal of these people was on racial or ancestral grounds only. World War II, the war against racism; yet no Germans or other enemy aliens were placed in protective custody. There should have been Japanese writers directing their writings toward Japanese audiences." (Yellow writings?)

Lee's poetry is—necessarily: imperatively—capable of an awful fang and of a massive beautifully awful supersedure.

From *Malcolm Spoke/who listened?:*
animals come in all colors.
dark meat will roast as fast as whi-te meat
especially in
the unitedstatesofamerica's
new
self-cleaning ovens.

if we don't listen.

From *The Revolutionary Screw:*
brothers,
i
under/overstand
the situation: . . . . . .

From *blackmusic/a beginning:*
paraoh sanders
had
finished
playing
&
the whi
te boy was to
go on next.

him didn't

him sd
his horn
was
broke.

And from *A Message All Blackpeople Can Dig:*

we'll move together
hands on weapons & families
blending into the sun,
into each/other.
we'll love,
we've always loved.
just be cool & help one/another.
go ahead.
walk a righteous direction
under the moon,
in the night
bring new meanings to
the north star,
to blackness,
to US.
discover new stars:
street-light stars that will explode into evil-eyes,
light-bulb stars visible only to the realpeople,
clean stars, african & asian stars,
black aesthetic stars that will damage the whi-te mind;
killer stars that will move against
the unpeople.

And always, in the center of acid, beauties that are not eaten
away!
   "The black writer learns from his people," says Don L.

81

Lee. ". . . Black artists are culture stabilizers, bringing back old values, and introducing new ones."

Poetry should—"allatonce"—distill, interpret, and extend. Don Lee's poetry does.

Black poets are the authentic poets of today. Recently, one of The Critics* opined (of white poets): ". . . it's hardly surprising to find a deep longing for death as the terrible sign of their self-respect and indeed the means by which they continue to live—if not as men, at least as poets." And on: "Although death may not be the resolution of everyone's problems, it is nevertheless the one poets wait and pray for. . . ."

Can you imagine Don Lee subscribing to any of this? Black poets do not subscribe to death. When choice is possible, they choose to die only in defense of life, in defense and in honor of life.

White poetry! Never has white technique-in-general been as scintillant and various. Never has less been said. Modern corruption and precise limpness, modern narcissism, nonsense, dry winter and chains have a grotesque but granular grip on the white verse of today.

Sometimes there is a quarrel. "Can poetry be 'black'? Isn't all poetry just POETRY?" The fact that a poet is black means that his life, his history and the histories of his ancestors have been different from the histories of Chinese and Japanese poets, Eskimo poets, Indian poets, Irish poets. The juice from tomatoes is not called merely *juice*. It is always called TOMATO juice. If you go into a restaurant desiring tomato juice you do not order the waiter to bring you "juice": you request, distinctly, TOMATO juice. The juice

---

* Jascha Kessler: "The Caged Sybil." *Saturday Review,* December 14, 1968.

from cranberries is called cranberry juice. The juice from oranges is called orange juice. The poetry from black poets is black poetry. Inside it are different nuances AND outrightnesses.

This is part of the decision of Don Lee—who is a further pioneer and a positive prophet, a prophet not afraid to be positive even though aware of a daily evolving, of his own sober and firm churning. He is a toughness. He is not a superficial toughness. He is the kind of toughness that doesn't just sass its mammy but goes right through to the bone.

Black Poetics/for the many to come

The most significant factor about the poems/poetry you will be reading is the *idea*. The *idea* is not the manner in which a poem is conceived but the conception itself. From the *idea* we move toward development & direction (direction: the focusing of yr/idea in a positive or negative manner; depending on the poet's orientation.) Poetic form is synonymous with poetic structure and is the guide used in developing yr/idea.

What u will be reading is blackpoetry. Blackpoetry is written for/to/about & around the lives/spiritactions/humanism & total existence of blackpeople. Blackpoetry in form/sound/word usage/intonation/rhythm/repetition/direction/definition & beauty is opposed to that which is now (& yesterday) considered poetry, i.e., whi-te poetry. Blackpoetry in its purest form is diametrically opposed to whi-te poetry. Whereas, blackpoets deal in the concrete rather than the abstract (concrete: art for people's sake; black language or Afro-american language in contrast to standard english, &c.). Blackpoetry moves to define & legitimize blackpeople's reality (*that* which is real to us.) Those in power (the unpeople) control and legitimize the negroes' (the realpeople's) reality out of that which they, the unpeople, consider real. That is, to the unpeople the television programs *Julia* and *The Mod Squad* reflect their vision of what they feel the blackman *is* about or *should* be about. So, in effect, blackpoetry is out to negate the negative influences of the mass media; whether it be TV, newspapers, magazines or some whi-te boy standing on a stage saying he's a "blue eyed soul brother."

Blackpeople must move to where all confrontations with the unpeople are meaningful and constructive. That means that most, if not all, blackpoetry will be *political*. I've often come across black artists (poets, painters, actors, writers, &c.) who feel that they and their work should be apolitical; not realizing that to be apolitical is *to be* political in a negative way for blackfolks. There is *no* neutral blackart; either it *is* or it *isn't,* period. To say that one is not political is as dangerous as saying, "by any means necessary," it's an "intellectual" cop-out, & niggers are copping-out as regularly as blades of grass in a New England suburb. Being political is also why the black artist is considered dangerous by those who rule, the unpeople. The black artist by defining and legitimizing his own reality becomes a positive force in the black community (just think of the results of Le Roi Jones (Ameer Baraka) writing the lyrics for the music of James Brown.) You see, *black* for the blackpoet is a way of life. And, his totalactions will reflect that blackness & he will be an example for his community rather than another contradictor.

Blackpoetry will continue to define what *is* and what isn't. Will tell what is *to be* & how to *be* it (or bes it.) Blackpoetry *is* and will continue to be an important factor in culture building. I believe Robert Hayden had culture building in mind when he wrote these lines in an early poem:

> It is time to call the children
> Into the evening quiet of the living-room
> And teach them the legends of their blood.

Blackpoetry is excellence & truth and will continue to seek such. Blackpoetry will move to expose & wipe-out that which is not necessary for our existence as a people. *As a people* is the only way we can endure and blacknation building must accelerate at top speed. Blackpoetry is Ornette Coleman teaching violin & the Supremes being black again. Blackpoetry is like a razor; it's sharp & will cut deep, not

86

out to wound but to kill the inactive blackmind. Like, my oldman used to pickup numbers and he seldom got caught & I'm faster than him; this is a fight with well defined borders & I know the side I'm ON. See u. Go head, now.

As-Salaam Alaikum
don l. lee

To the keen clamour of the Negro from Africa to the
    Americas
It is the sign of the dawn
The sign of brotherhood which comes to nourish the
    dreams of men.

From the poem *Listen Comrades* by David Diop

In a land where the way of life is understood
Race-horses are led back to serve the field;
In a land where the way of life is not understood
War-horses are bred on the autumn yield.

There is no need to run outside
For better seeing,
Nor to peer from a window. Rather abide
At the center of your being;
For the more you leave it, the less you learn.
Search your heart and see
If he is wise who takes each turn:
The way to do is to be.

From *The Way of Life* According to Lao Tzu

The black artist. The black man. The holy holy black
man. The man you seek. The climber the striver. The maker
of peace. The lover. The warrior. We are they whom you
seek. Look in. Find yr self. Find the being, the speaker. The
voice, the black dust hover in your soft eyeclosings. Is you.
Is the creator. Is nothing. Plus or minus, you vehicle! We
are presenting. Your various selves. We are presenting, from
God, a tone, your own. Go on. Now.

From the FOREWORD to *Black Fire*,
Le Roi Jones (Ameer Baraka)

Gwendolyn Brooks

she doesn't wear
costume jewelry
& she knew that walt disney
was/is making a fortune off
false-eyelashes and that time magazine is the
authority on the knee/grow.
her makeup is total-real.

a negro english instructor called her:
        "a fine negro poet."
a whi-te critic said:
        "she's a credit to the negro race."
somebody else called her:
        "a pure negro writer."
johnnie mae, who's a senior in high school said:
        "she & langston are the only negro poets we've
        read in school and i understand her."
pee wee used to carry one of her poems around in his back
    pocket;
        the one about being cool. that was befo pee wee
        was cooled by a cop's warning shot.

into the sixties
a word was born .... BLACK
& with black came poets
& from the poet's ball points came:
black doubleblack purpleblack blueblack beenblack was
black daybeforeyesterday blackerthan ultrablack super
black blackblack yellowblack niggerblack blackwhi-teman
blackerthanyoueverbes ¼ black unblack coldblack clear
black my momma's blackerthanyourmomma pimpleblack fall
black so black we can't even see you black on black in

89

black by black technically black mantanblack winter
black coolblack 360degreesblack coalblack midnight
black black when it's convenient rustyblack moonblack
black starblack summerblack electronblack spaceman
black shoeshineblack jimshoeblack underwearblack ugly
black auntjimammablack, uncleben'srice black williebest
black blackisbeautifulblack i justdiscoveredblack negro
black unsubtanceblack.

and everywhere the
lady "negro poet"
appeared the poets were there.
they listened and questioned
& went home feeling uncomfortable/unsound & sounto-
    gether
they read/re-read/wrote & re-wrote
& came back the next time to tell the
lady "negro poet"
how beautiful she was/is & how she had helped them
& she came back with:
    how necessary they were and how they've helped her.
the poets walked & as space filled the vacuum between
    them & the
lady "negro poet"
u could hear one of the blackpoets say:
    "bro, they been calling that sister by the wrong name."

But He Was Cool
or: he even stopped for green lights

 super-cool
 ultrablack
 a tan/purple
 had a beautiful shade.

he had a double-natural
that wd put the sisters to shame.
his dashikis were tailor made
& his beads were imported sea shells
      (from some blk/country i never heard of)
he was triple-hip.

his tikis were hand carved
out of ivory
& came express from the motherland.
he would greet u in swahili
& say good-by in yoruba.
woooooooooooo-jim he bes so cool & ill tel li gent
                cool-cool is so cool he was un-cooled by
                        other niggers' cool
                cool-cool ultracool was bop-cool/ice box
                        cool so cool cool cool
                his wine didn't have to be cooled, him was
                        air conditioned cool
                cool-cool/real cool made me cool—now
                        ain't that cool
                cool-cool so cool him nick-named refrig-
                        erator.

cool-cool so cool
he didn't know,
after detroit, newark, chicago &c.,
we had to hip
            cool-cool/super-cool/real cool
        that
to be black
is
to be
very-hot.

Communication in Whi-te

dee dee dee dee dee wee weee eeeee wee we
deweeeeeeee ee ee ee nig

nig nig nig niggggggggg gg gggggggg cleek cleek cleek
cleeeeee cleekcleek

rip rip rip rip rip/rip/rip/rip/rip/ripripripripripripripri
pi pi pi pi pip

bom bom bom bom bom/bom/bom/bombombombom
bombbombbombbombbombbomb

deathtocleekdeathtocleekdeathtocleekdeathtocleek
deathtocleekdeathtodeathto

alllllllllllalllllllllll alllllllllll deathtoalllllllll alllllllll
alllllllleeeeeeee

te te te te te te te/te/te/te/te/te/ tetetetetetetetetete
tetetetetetete:
the paris peace talks, 1968.

93

Don't Cry, Scream

(for John Coltrane/from a black poet/
in a basement apt. crying dry tears of
"you ain't gone.)

into the sixties
a trane
came/out of the
fifties with a
golden boxcar
riding the rails
of novation.
      blowing
      a-melodics
      screeching,
      screaming,
      blasting—
         driving some away,
         (those paper readers who thought
         manhood was something innate)

         bring others in,
         (the few who didn't believe that the
         world existed around established whi
         teness & leonard bernstein)
music that ached.
murdered our minds (we reborn)
born into a neoteric aberration.
& suddenly
you envy the
BLIND man—
you know that he will
hear what you'll never
see.

94

your music is like
my head—nappy black/
a good nasty feel with
tangled songs of:

    we-eeeeeeeeeee   sing
    WE-EEEeeeeeeeeee   loud &
    WE-EEEEEEEEEEEEEEEEEE   high
                                        with
                                        feeling

a people playing
the sound of me when
i combed it. combed at
it.

i cried for billy holiday.
the blues. we ain't blue
the blues exhibited illusions of manhood.
destroyed by you. Ascension into:
    scream-eeeeeeeeeeeeee-ing   sing
    SCREAM-EEEeeeeeeeeeee-ing   loud &
    SCREAM-EEEEEEEEEEEEEE-ing long with
                                        feeling

we ain't blue, we are black.
we ain't blue, we are black.
      (all the blues did was
      make me cry)
soultrane gone on a trip
he left man images
he was a life-style of
man-maker & annihilator
of attache case carriers.

Trane done went.
(got his hat & left me one)
naw brother,
i didn't cry,
i just—

Scream-eeeeeeeeeeeeeeee-ed   sing loud
 SCREAM-EEEEEEEEEEEEEEEEEE-ED   & high with
  we-eeeeeeeeeeeeeeeeeeee eeee ee   feeling
  WE-EEEEEEeeeeeeeeeEEEEEEEE   letting
  WE-EEEEEEEEEEEEEEEEEEEEEEEE   yr/voice
  WHERE YOU DONE GONE, BROTHER? break

it hurts, grown babies
dying. born. done caught me
a trane. steel wheels broken
by popsicle sticks. i went out
& tried to buy a nickle bag
with my standard oil card.

            (swung on a faggot who politely
            scratched his ass in my presence.
            he smiled broken teeth stained from
            his over-used tongue. fisted-face.
            teeth dropped in tune with ray
            charles singing "yesterday.")

blonds had more fun—
with snagga-tooth niggers
who saved pennies & pop bottles for week-ends
to play negro & other filthy inventions.
be-bop-en to james brown's
cold sweat—these niggers didn't sweat,
they perspired. & the blond's dye came out,
i ran. she did too, with his pennies, pop bottles

& his mind. tune in next week same time same station
for anti-self in one lesson.

to the negro cow-sissies
who did tchaikovsky &
the beatles & live in
split-level homes & had
split-level minds & babies.
who committed the act of
love with their clothes on.
> (who hid in the bathroom to read
> jet mag., who didn't read the chicago
> defender because of the misspelled
> words & had shelves of books by
> europeans on display. untouched. who
> hid their little richard & lightin'
> slim records & asked: "John who?"

>   instant hate.)
they didn't know any better,
brother, they were too busy getting
into debt, expressing humanity &
taking off color.
  SCREAMMMM/we-eeeee/screech/teee   improvise
  aheeeeeeeee/screeeeeee/theeee/ee   with
  ahHHHHHHHHH/WEEEEEEEE/scrEEE   feeling
        EEEE
     we-eeeeeWE-EEEEEEEWE-EE-EEEEE

the ofays heard you &
were wiped out. spaced.
one clown asked me during,
my favorite things, if
you were practicing.

i fired on the muthafucka & said,
"i'm practicing."
naw brother,
i didn't cry.
i got high off my thoughts—
they kept coming back,
back to destroy me.

& that BLIND man
i don't envy anymore
i can see his hear
& hear his heard through my pores.
i can see my me. it was truth you gave,
like a daily shit
it had to come.

        can you scream—brother?   very
        can you scream—brother?   soft

i hear you.
i hear you.

and the Gods will too.

Assassination

it was wild.
the
bullet hit high
          (the throat-neck)

& from everywhere:
          the motel, from under bushes and cars,
          from around corners and across streets,
          out of the garbage cans and from rat holes
          in the earth
they came running.
with
guns
drawn
they came running
toward the King—
               all of them
               fast and sure—
as if
the King
was going to fire back.
they came running,
fast and sure,
in the
wrong
direction.

Malcolm Spoke/who listened?
(this poem is for my consciousness too)

he didn't say
wear yr/blackness in
outer garments
& blk/slogans fr/the top 10.

he was fr a long
line of super-cools,
    doo-rag lovers &
    revolutionary pimps.
u are playing that
high-yellow game in blackface
minus the straighthair.
now
it's nappy-black
& air conditioned volkswagens
with undercover whi
te girls who studied faulkner at
smith
& are authorities on "militant"
knee/grows
selling u at jew town rates:
    niggers with wornout tongues
    three for a quarter/or will consider a trade

the double-breasted hipster
has been replaced with a
dashiki wearing rip-off
who went to city college
majoring in physical education.

animals come in all colors.
dark meat will roast as fast as whi-te meat
especially in
the unitedstatesofamerica's
new
self-cleaning ovens.

if we don't listen.

From a Black Perspective

wallace for president
his momma for vice-president

was scribbled
on the men's room wall
on
over
the toilet

where
it's
supposed to be.

Blackrunners/blackmen
or run into blackness
(for brothers tommie smith & john carlos—
super-sprinters—but most of all blackmen)

u beat them
brothers;
at their own game.
(out-ran the world-runners)
whi-te boys
& others
had a dust-meal.

u beat them.
now
in this time in space
the rule-makers
are also
the vanquished.

anyhow/way
we can't eat gold medals
& sportsmanship is racism
in three syllables.

u beat them brothers
and u/we
will beat them again.
they
just don't know
that
u've/got friends
&
we know how to
fight dirty.

103

A Poem to Complement Other Poems

change.
like if u were a match i wd light u into something beauti-
    ful. change.
change.
for the better into a realreal together thing. change, from
    a make believe
nothing on corn meal and water. change.
change. from the last drop to the first, maxwellhouse
    did. change.
change was a programmer for IBM, thought him was a
    brown computor. change.
colored is something written on southern out-
    houses. change.
greyhound did, i mean they got rest rooms on buses.
    change.
change.
change nigger.
saw a nigger hippy, him wanted to be different. changed.
saw a nigger liberal, him wanted to be different.
    changed.
saw a nigger conservative, him wanted to be different.
    changed.
niggers don't u know that niggers are different. change.
a doublechange. nigger wanted a double zero in front of
    his name; a license to kill,
niggers are licensed to be killed. change. a negro: some-
    thing pigs eat.
change. i say change into a realblack righteous aim. like
    i don't play
saxophone but that doesn't mean i don't dig 'trane.'
    change.

change.
hear u coming but yr/steps are too loud. change. even a
lamp post changes nigger.
change, stop being an instant yes machine. change.
niggers don't change they just grow. that's a change;
bigger & better niggers.
change, into a necessary blackself.
change, like a gas meter gets higher.
change, like a blues song talking about a righteous to-
morrow.
change, like a tax bill getting higher.
change, like a good sister getting better.
change, like knowing wood will burn. change.
know the realenemy.
change,
change nigger: standing on the corner, thought him was
cool. him still
standing there. it's winter time, him cool.
change,
know the realenemy.
change: him wanted to be a TV star. him is. ten o'clock
news.
wanted, wanted. nigger stole some lemon & lime
popsicles,
thought them were diamonds.
change nigger change.
know the realenemy.
change: is u is or is u aint. change. now now change. for
the better change.
read a change. live a change. read a blackpoem.
change. be the realpeople.
change. blackpoems
will change:

History of the Poet As a Whore
(to all negro poets who deal in whi-te paronomasia)

yeats in brown-tone
ultrablack with whi-te tan,
had a dangerous notion that
he/she
wd be famous yesterday.
a paper prostitute
with ink stained contraceptions.
still,
accute fear of colored pregnancy
forces poet to be poet
& not "negro poet" (supposedly a synonym for blk/poet)
whose poem-poems are conceived in
nine month intevals
with a
rarity of miscarriages tho most are
premature.
whereas R.A.M.* becomes
royal academy of music
& another poet's poem
aid in
mental genocide of blackpeople
while
he/she switches down the
street with
his/her ass wide-open bleeding
whi-te blood.

------

*Revolutionary Action Movement

A Poem for Negro Intellectuals
(if there bes such a thing)

&
blackwoman be ahead
moved
un-noticed
throughout the
world
a people deathliving
in
abstract realities
hoping/looking
for
blk/man-actions
from
action-livers.

&
blackmen,
action-givers to the
world
unknown to
yr/own

will
unlike yes
terday
again
be born into
a
blk/self.

u
will move

as swift as
black d.c. sevens
or as
sharprazors fr/blk/hands
swinging
among mid-night stars
where
everything is
in
place
as it was
yes
    terday &
yes
    terday &
yes
it will not be so tomorrow,
if we do.

Nigerian Unity/
Or Little Niggers Killing Little Niggers
(for brothers Christopher Okigbo & Wole Soyinka)

suppose those
who made
wars
had to fight them?

it's called blackgold.
& you,
my brothers/former warriors
who use to own the nights
that
knew no boarders
have acquired strings on yr/minds
& have knowingly sold yr/our/mothers.
there are no more tears.
tears will not stop bullets.
the dead don't cry,
the dead just grow; good crop this year,
wouldn't u say.

it's called blackgold
& u fight blindly,
swinging at yr/own mid-nights
at yr/own children of tomorrow.

come   one   come   two
against the middle is
a double feature starring the man from u.n.c.l.e.
with a nigger on his back
who played ping-pong with christ
and won.

little niggers
killing
little niggers: ontime/intime/outoftime
                 theirtime/otherpeople'stime as
                 niggers killed niggers everytime.

suppose those
who made
wars
had to fight them?

blackgold is not
the newnigger:
with a british accent
called me 'old chap' one day,
i rubbed his skin
it didn't come off. even him surprised.

him
another pipe-smoking faggot
who lost his balls in
a double-breasted suit
walking thru a nadinola commercial
with a degree in european history.
little nigger
choked himself with a hippy's tie
his momma didn't even know him/
                 she thought he was a TWA flashback or
                 something out of a polka-dot machine.

he
cursed at her in perfect english
called her:
Mother-Dear.

WANTED   WANTED
          black warriors to go south
          to fight in Africa's mississippi.

go south young man.

everybody missed that train,
except one sister.
she wanted to fight the realenemy
but
she was "uneducated,"
wore the long-dress
talked the native tongue
& had a monopoly on blackbeauty.
when we met—she smiled & said: "i'm the true gold,
                                    i'm the real-gold."

suppose those
who made
wars
had to fight them?

the real blackgold
was there before the drill,
before the dirty-eyed,
before the fence-builders,
before the wells,
before the british accent,
before christ,
before air condition,
before the cannon,
the real blackgold: was momma & sister; is momma &
    sister.
was there before the "educated,"
before the pig-eaters,

111

before the cross-wearers,
before the pope,
before the nigger-warriors.
the real blackgold
was the first warrior.

go south young man.

little niggers
killing
little niggers.
the weak against the weak.
the ugly against the ugly.
the powerless against the powerless.
the realpeople becoming unpeople
& brothers we have more in common
than pigmentation & stupidity.
that same old two-for-one
was played on 47th & ellis—
invented on 125th & lenox
and now is double-dealing from
the mangrove swamps to the savannah grassland;
2 niggers for the price of nothing.

newnigger
lost his way
a whi-te girl gave him direction
him still lost
she sd whi-te/he thought bite
been eating everything in sight
including himself.

suppose those
who made
wars

had to fight them?

the lone ranger got a new tonto
he's 'brown' with a Ph.D. in
psy-chol-o-gy
& still walks around with
holes
in his brain.
losthismind.

saw him the other day
with his head across some railroad tracks—
tryin to get an untan.
will the real jesus christ
please stand up
and take a bow;
u got niggers tryin to be trains.

trained well.
european-african took a
double
at oxford.
wears ban-lon underwear & whi-te socks,
has finally got the killer's eye,
join the deathbringers club
& don't want more than two children.

the real blackgold
will be crippled,
raped,
and killed
in
that
order.

i will miss
the joy
of calling her
sister

go south young man.

suppose those
who made
wars
had to fight *you*.

Blackmusic/ A Beginning

        pharaoh sanders
        had
        finished
        playing
        &
        the whi-
        te boy was to
        go on next.

        him didn't

        him sd
        that
        his horn
        was
        broke.

        they sat
        there
        dressed in
        african garb
        & dark sun glasses
        listening to the brothers
        play.   (taking notes)

        we
        didn't realize
        who they
        were un
        til their
        next recording
        had been

released: the beach boys play soulmusic.

real sorry about
the supremes
being dead,
heard some whi
te girls
the other day—
all wigged-down
with a mean tan—
soundin just like them,
singin
rodgers & hart
& some country & western.

Black Sketches

1

i
was five
when
mom & dad got married
& i
didn't realize that
i
was illegitimate
until i started
school.

2

i was at
the airport
& had
to use the
men's room
real bad
& didn't have a
dime.

3

somebody
made a
mistake (they said)
&
sent the
peace corps to
europe.

4

went to cash
my
1968 tax refund
&
the check bounced;
insufficient funds.

5

i
read the
newspapers today
&
thought that
everything
was
all right.

6

nat turner
returned
&
killed
william styron
&
his momma too.

7

ed brooke
sat at his
desk
crying & slashing
his wrist
because somebody
called him
black.

8

general westmoreland
was transferred
to the
westside of chicago
&
he lost
there too.

9

in 1959
my mom
was dead at the
age of
35
& nobody thought it unusual
not even
me.

10
in 1963
i
became black
& everyone thought it unusual;
even me.

11
the american dream:
> nigger bible in
> every hotel;
> iceberg slim (pimp) getting
> next to julia;
> & roy wilkins on
> the mod squad.

✳ blackwoman:

will define herself. naturally. will
talk/walk/live/& love her images. her
beauty will be. the only way to be is
to be. blackman take her. u don't need
music to move; yr/movement toward her
is music. & she'll do more than dance.

✳ BLACKWOMAN

blackwoman:
is an
in and out
rightsideup
action-image
of her man. . . . .
in other
(blacker) words;
she's together,
if
he
bes.

The Third World Bond
(for my sisters & their sisters)

            they were
            blk/revolutionist.
            & they often talked
            of the third world
            & especially of the power
            of
            china.
                    (quoting mao every 3rd word)
            they were
            revolutionist
            & the blk/sisters knew it
            & looked,
            & wondered
            while the brothers/
            the revolutionists,
            made bonds
            with the
            3rd world
            thru
            chinese women.
            the sisters waited.
            (& wondered when the revolution would start)

122

The Revolutionary Screw
(for my blacksisters)

    brothers,
    i
    under/overstand
    the situation:

    i mean—
        u bes hitten the man hard
        all day long.
    a stone revolutionary, "a full time revolutionary."
        tellen the man how bad u is
        & what u goin ta do
        & how u goin ta do it.

    it must be a bitch
    to be able to do all that
    talken. (& not one irregular breath fr/yr/mouth)
    being so
    forceful & all
    to the man's face (the courage)
    & u not even cracken a smile (realman.)

    i know,
    the sisters just don't
    understand the
    pressure u is under.

    &
    when u ask for a piece
    of leg/
    it's not for yr/self
    but for
    yr/people————it keeps u going

& anyway u is a revolutionary
& she wd be doin
a revolutionary thing.

that sister dug it
from the beginning,
had an early-eye.
i mean
she really had it together
when she said:
        go fuck yr/self nigger.
now
that was
revolutionary.

Reflections on a Lost Love
(for my brothers who think they are lovers
and my sisters who are the real-lovers)

        back in chi/
        all the blackwomen
        are fine.
        super fine.
        even the ones who:
                dee bob/ de bop/ she-shoo-bop
                bop de-bop/ dee dee bop/ dee-she-dee-she-bop
                we-We eeeeeeeeeeeeeee/ WEEEEEEEEEEEEEEE
        they so fine/
        that
        when i slide up
        to one & say: take it off   sing
                        take it off   slow
                             take it all off   with feeling

        & she would say: "if i doos,
                        does u think u can groove dad—dy"
        & i wd say: "can chitlins smell,
                    is toejam black,
                    can a poet, poet,
                    can a musician, music?"
                weeeee/ weeeeeee/ de-bop-a-dee-bop
                whooo-bop/ dee-bop a-she-bop

as she smiled
& unbuttoned that top button
i sd: take it off   sing
          take it off   slow
                take it off   with feeling

first the skirt,
then the blouse
& next her wig (looked like she made it herself)
next the shoes & then
the eyelashes and jewelry
&
          dee-bop/bop-a-ree-bop/WOW
the slip
& next the bra (they weren't big, but that didn't scare
     me)
cause i was grooven now: dee/dee-bop-a-she-bop/
          weeeeeEEEEEEEEEE
as she moved to the most important part,
i got up & started to groove myself but my eyes stopped
     me.
first her stockens down those shapely legs—
followed by black bikini panties, that just slid down
and
i just stood—
& looked with utter amazement as she said: in a deep
                    "hi baby—my name is   man-like
                    joe sam."   voice

A Poem Looking for a Reader
(to be read with a love consciousness)

black is not
all inclusive,
there are other colors.
color her warm and womanly,
color her feeling and life,
color her a gibran poem & 4 women of simone.
children will give her color
paint her the color of her
man.

most of all color her
love
a remembrance of life
a truereflection
that we
will
move   u will move with
i want
u
a fifty minute call to blackwomanworld:
       hi baby,
       how u doin?

need u.
listening to
young-holt's, *please sunrise, please.*

to give   i'll give
most personal.
what about the other
scenes: children playing in vacant lots,

or like the first time u knowingly kissed a girl,
was it joy or just beautifully beautiful.
i
remember at 13
reading chester himes'
cast the first stone and
the eyes of momma when she caught me: read on, son.
how will u come:
    like a soulful strut in a two-piece beige o-rig'-i-nal,
    or afro-down with a beat in yr/walk?
how will love come:
    painless and deep like a razor cut
    or like some cheap 75c movie;
    i think not.

will she be the woman
other men will want
or
will her beauty be
accented with my name on it?

she will come as she would
want her man to come.
she'll come,
she'll come.
i
never wrote a love letter
but
that doesn't mean
i
don't love.

A Message All Blackpeople Can Dig
(& a few negroes too)

    we are going to do it.
    US: blackpeople, beautiful people; the sons and daugh-
       ters of beautiful people.
    bring it back to
    US: the unimpossibility.
    now is
    the time, the test
    while there is something to save (other than our lives).

    we'll move together
    hands on weapons & families
    blending into the sun,
    into each/other.
    we'll love,
    we've always loved.
    just be cool & help one/another.
    go ahead.
    walk a righteous direction
    under the moon,
    in the night
    bring new meanings to
    the north star,
    the blackness,
    to US.

discover new stars:
street-light stars that will explode into evil-eyes,
light-bulb stars visible only to the realpeople,
clean stars, african & asian stars,
black aestheic stars that will damage the whi-temind;
killer stars that will move against
the unpeople.

come
brothers/fathers/sisters/mothers/sons/daughters
dance as one
walk slow and hip.
hip to what life is
and can be.
& remember we are not hippies,
WE WERE BORN HIP.
walk on. smile a little
yeah, that's it beautiful people
move on in, take over. take over, take over take/over
      takeovertakeovertakeover
   takeovertakeover overtakeovertakeovertake over/
      take over take, over take,
    over   take,   over   take.
blackpeople
are moving, moving to return
      this earth into the hands of

human beings.

We Walk theWay of the New World

1969-1970

your enemy
knows
his enemy

DEDICATION
or to those
who helped create a New Consciousness

William E. B. Du Bois, Carter G. Woodson,
J. A. Rogers, Lerone Bennett:
> to them history is not a weak re-writing of pro-black-
> ness, but a complete re-interpretation with the proper
> perspective. their vision put them among the history-
> poets of the *New World.*

Wallace Thurman,
Claude McKay, James Weldon Johnson:
> Harlem & blackness to them was more than white
> boys dropping money to print bad books. they left us
> something meaningful to grow on.

Richard Wright,
Paul Robeson, E. Franklin Frazier:
> the dynamiters. makers of new words/ ideas that did
> more than just walk the page, they jumped at us with
> unrelenting force that wdn't wait.

Kwame Nkrumah, Patrice Lumumba,
Sekou Touré, Julius K. Nyerere:
> makers of the *New World,* Africa. made us realize that
> *we're an African people.* . . . . . .

Frantz Fanon:
> taught us a new psychology, we're still learning.

Miriam Makeba, Nina Simone:
> two internationally known blackwomen entertainers
> that are consistently black & relevant, can u name me
> two brothers/blackmen that are as . . . .

132

Lew Alcindor:
> tomorrow's athlete. a blackman first & a ball player second. rite-on Lew, righteously.

Waring Cuney, Aimé Césaire:
> poets who knew, and said it.

Katherine Dunham:
> a lady who danced & danced & danced.

and
to all movement women:
> soft. indestructible. warm. sure. true. as they watched their men marry the women who were not there. they sacrificed much.

The highest art is that which awakens our dormant will-force and nerves us to face the trials of life naturally. All that brings drowsiness and makes us shut our eyes to Reality around, on the mastery of which alone Life depends, is a message of decay and death. There should be no opiumeating in Art. The dogma of Art for the sake of Art is a clever invention of decadence to cheat us of life and power

—*Allama Muhammad Iqbal*

INTRODUCTION: Louder but Softer

Yesterday is not today. What was visible in the old books is *still there,* that's why new ones are written. Yesterday's light was bright and lived suspended within its own energy. Today the only time we see it is by traveling 35,000 feet above the earth at some ridiculous speed; our children will not know the *sun* as we knew it, but will appreciate it more.

We're talking about our children, a survival of a people. A people can't possibly survive if they become something else. The process of change, of reconditioning a people to be something other than themselves started centuries ago: we used to be blackmen/women (or Africans); now we're known as *negroes.* That movement toward becoming an adjective was not accidental; but carefully planned and immaculately executed to completely rape a people of their culture. Whereas, most of us have become another man's imagination, a reflection of another man's fantasy, a nonentity, a filthy invention. So, in effect we'll be talking about definitions & change. When we say definitions, we mean the present and the past with the proper perspective. Understand that *objectivity* is a *myth,* where "one makes judgments in terms of one's culture and in keeping with the cultural values which are a part of his personal and immediate heritage. These cultural values depend for their duration upon the survival of the classes which created them." *Change* is to be that, an on-going process aimed at an ultimate definition of our being. But when we talk about change, we don't mean from *Winston* to *Marlboro.* Actually, we mean from negative to positive, from the creative to the anti-cliché.

What is meant is that we'll have to move from imitation to initiation; from number one to number first; from the Tonight Show to our own Lenox Avenue where

brothers shadow box with wind because the wind is the
only element that will touch them. Check it out, if u
ain't scared to venture back.

Can you believe in yourself? It's not enough to say *I'm Somebody:* we've always known that. The question *is* who/ what? Are you a dead raindrop, reborn in a used coal mine now existing in an oblique closet of your closed mind, only to re-emerge singing "I'm black and I'm proud" while soft peddling *before* the jew into the new self-cleaning ovens. After all, it takes little or no work to be insignificant, but to leave our print, our image on the world, you'll find that 24 hours in a day is like seconds in a fast minute.

The rejection of that which was/is ours has been the basis for the acceptance of that which is someone else's. The most effective weapon used against us has been the educational system. We now understand that if *white nationalism* is our teacher, *white nationalism* will be our philosophy regardless of *all* its contradictory and anti-black implications. The educational process is set up largely to preserve that which *is,* not that which necessarily needs to be created, i.e., black nationalism or black consciousness. Thus we find ourselves trying to determine which are the correct answers for future development. Some of the answers will have to be a surprise, but at least we know a surprise is coming.

In the late sixties we existed in a state of *cultural nihilism,* and the destruction that came was mainly against our own in our own. Destruction and mis-direction became the overwhelming directives. Positive influences existed in the sixties and before, but their accessibility was limited to the few. So we moved, traveling speedily from one consciousness to another, hoping that our actions would not betray our movement. Blackness as we speak of it today is nothing

137

new; other writers at other times wrote about themselves and their people as we do now. The main difference, if there has to be one, is the audience which the writers directed their voices toward. Black writers—from the first and up into the sixties—have largely (with few exceptions) followed the trend of *being* or becoming "American writers," not *negro* writers but writers who happened to be *negro*. All that is in the process of being erased. We discovered a new psychology. The sixties brought us the work of one Frantz Fanon and his powerful *The Wretched of the Earth* and other books: the Honorable Elijah Muhammad, the prophet of the Nation of Islam, ultimately produced the loudest and clearest voice for the young blacks through Al Hajj Malik al Shabazz, better known as Malcolm X, who in turn moved us toward a national consciousness. He heavily influenced a writer who proved to be a consistent bullet in the side of white America—Imamu Amiri Baraka (LeRoi Jones).

> *What does it take to reach you, into you? What is the stimulus that will force you to act; what motivates you in yr inability to conceive of yrself as something special? Will it take the death of a loved one? Will the values you consider valuable have to be destroyed? Is the knowledge of self so painful as to demand that you not accept it and continue to squalor in yr naiveté?*

Culture is the sustaining force of any nation. An effective con game has been played on black people in this country. We've been taught to be anti-black, anti-self. No need in documenting that, for all one has to do is walk in any black neighborhood and if you possess only an ounce of perception, the examples will fly at you. We are the only people in a nation of many people who have consistently let others guide

138

us. We've been so busy taking directions from others that our ability to conceive of ourselves as direction-givers has not had a chance to flourish. However, others—those that traditionally have led us—recognized our revolutionary potential. Harold Cruse puts it this way: "They understood it *instinctively,* (the Negro's white radical allies) and revolutionary theory had little to do with it. What . . . the Negro's allies feared most of all was that this sleeping, dream-walking black giant might wake up and direct the revolution all by himself, relegating his white allies to a humiliating, second-class status. The Negro's allies were not about to tell the Negro anything that might place him on the path to greater power and independence in the revolutionary movement than they themselves had. The rules of the power game meant that unless the American Negro taught himself the profound implications of his own revolutionary significance in America, it would never be taught to him by anyone else." We black people in America are not culturally deprived, but "culturally different"; actually we're products of a dual culture, having the benefits and evils of the dominant WASPS and our own unique Afro-Americanism. Here we are, about 30 million voices (larger than some nations) coming into a new decade, still not fully cognizant of the ultimate reality of our power, if only in sheer numbers.

"Almost daily, small bands of Jewish arrivals tramp up the gangplank of the Saint Lawrence, *the hotel ship acquired by the Danish Refugee Council to house them temporarily . . . 'You must understand,' a recently arrived 40 year old female physician said. 'Our world has been shattered. My husband and I . . . had almost forgotten that we were Jews; we were simply Poles. But then someone denounced us.' . . . The doctor and her husband—*

who is also a physician—were . . . accused of hiding their 'Jewishness.'"

—*Newsweek,* January 12, 1970

The theater was Poland, the former homeland of more than three million Jews, reduced to 75,000 after Hitler's Aryan society came into power, and today Poland contains less than 15,000. The year is 1970 and the issues are the same, *race.* We can continue to cloud our direction with meaningless rhetoric and romantic illusions, but when it comes down to the deathwalk, no one will save a people but the people themselves. Let's look at the Jewish and black situations here, since Jews and blacks are among the largest "minority" groups.

How can less than six million American Jews be more effective than Afro-Americans that outnumber them almost five to one. The watchword is culture and a steady "survival motion." The Jewish people have a tradition of togetherness and peoplehood. They've developed a nationalist conscious-ness that's interwoven with their religious reality. They've developed life-giving and life-saving institutions. They've developed the sophistication for survival. If a Jew hates you, you'll never know it; if he plans to kill you, you know even less: Sophistication. They recognized years ago that *Mission Impossible* and *James Bond* are for real. So, how does one compete with such impossible odds without inviting suicide? Simple, yet difficult. You become a nation within a nation. You create and sustain your own identity. In effect, Jewish teachers teach Jewish children, especially in the primary levels; Jewish doctors administer aid to Jewish patients (and others); the Jewish business world services the Jewish com-munity; and each sector continually draws on one another to build that community. Rabbi Zev Segal, head of the country's largest and most influential Jewish Orthodox rabbinical group, estimated that close to one hundred million dollars has been spent annually in the last few years on Jewish educational institutions; he also goes on to say that Jewish education is necessary for the survival of Judaism. Also, he and others *rightly feel* that they face "physical danger" if they as a people cannot remain as a people. Thus, Rabbi Segal feels that the Jewish schools are the "core institutions for Jewish survival and identity."

Elsewhere I've said that if all you are exposed to is Charlie Chan, you'll have a Charlie Chan mentality. A better example is Tarzan. Remember Tarzan grew out of one man's imagination, but because of prevailing anti-black conditions, he immediately became a nation's consciousness. What Tarzan did was not only to turn us away from Africa, but from ourselves. And that's where we are now, still unsure of ourselves, walking after somebody else's dreams, while the only fighting being waged is within the race. The killing of each other is not a test for manhood. But manhood has not been defined. And our survival will ultimately be determined by the will or non-will of black men—it will not be an over night process and we see that our most important asset is the next/ and present generation of black college students.

Stop!

Black student after winter vacation on his way back to school (University of America) a part of the Jet set. I wouldn't have noticed him, but he was dressed rather oddly; along with about a five inch natural he had an Indian band around his forehead; with a gold ear-ring in his left ear. A black tiki hung around his neck partially hid under a red and green scarf that loosely covered an orange dashiki that housed a black turtle neck sweater. His tailor made white bell bottoms were accented by brown buckled cowboy boots while a black slick-haired fur coat rested on his right arm looking like it could bite. Now, here we have a brother that didn't know what he was, an international nigger— you name it, he'll be a part of it. As I approached him, his first words after "What's happnin, baby," were "do you smoke, bro."

Stop!

Time is not new; it must be on our side, we're still here. Send young black brothers and sisters to college and they come home Greeks, talking about they can't relate to the community anymore. So here we have black Alpha Phi Alpha, Delta Sigma Theta, etc., unable to speak Greek, with an obvious non-knowledge of Greek culture—only supported by an ignorance of their own past (or present); only, after four years, to be graduated as some of the best whist players since the Cincinatti Kid who didn't finish high school.

Today's black college students fall into two categories: the serious and the unserious. By the unserious I mean the lesser but growing portion of black students who attend today's universities with the attitude that they are "students" and nothing else. Whereas being a "student" implies superficial intellectuality that borders on hipness—that is, being hip enough to be able to quote all the current writers to impress those who are impressed by that; very little study (that's for squares, u a brain anyhow); a lot of partying (with the 3 R's of reading, riting, and rithmetic being replaced with *ripple, reefers,* and *rappin'*); and a possession of the attitude that "I got mine, you get yours" or "every man for himself," so there exists no real commitment to themselves, or to their people. And lastly we have the student who will say that *all* the courses are irrelevant—not realizing it's going to take some of that irrelevance to put us in a position for survival.

Finally, we have the serious student who is not only committed to himself, but to his people. Students who realize that they come to college as black men or women will come out as doctors, lawyers, teachers, historians, writers, etc., who are black, and *not* doctors, lawyers, teachers, historians, writers, etc., who happen to be black. No, you are blackmen and women who are black first and products of your vocation second—therefore understanding our priorities. These are New World students who are in the process of developing the necessary group consciousness, nationalistic consciousness or black consciousness that is absolutely necessary for real development.

You as black students will become the new heroes for our children; will move to replace the pimps, prostitutes and wineheads who are now viewed as heroes because of no meaningful alternative. A part of your responsibility will be to change a rather complex and growing situation in our communities. Think about it, be for real about realness; it's not for the community to relate to you, you relate to that which you left. The community is still there—unchanged. You have changed; the question is how? Please, don't space on us just because you think you're educated now. Don't become the *new* pimps, educated pimps existing as a creation of your own mind, unwilling to share with anyone because you think it's *too deep*. Try us, you may not be as deep as you think you are. Stop romanticizing your existence, stop romanticizing the black revolution. Like Brother Malcolm said, *"if you really understood revolution, you wouldn't even use the term,"* or as a sister put it—all the revolutionaries

143

she knew were either *dead* or off quietly planning somewhere. Need I say more?

So we say, move into yr own self, Clean. If we were as together as our music and dancing, we'd be a trip in itself. Can you dig that, if we were as up tight as our dancing and music, we wouldn't have a worry except how to stay new and inventive. For an example, take our music. It is commonly accepted that it is the *only* cultural form that is uniquely American—that is, not an off-shoot of European culture. But still, we don't control our own contributions— the money makers have not been the black musicians but the producers and record companies. What is even worse is that our music is being stolen each and every day and passed off as another's creation—take Tom Jones and Janis Joplin, two white performers who try to sing black. They've not only become rich, while black musicians starve in their own creation, but those two whites, plus others—who are at best poor copies of what they consider black—will after a short period of time become the *standard*. It will get to the point where when you speak of *soul* and black music, you will find people automatically thinking of white imitators.

We now find ourselves in the seventies and cannot possibly use the tactics of the sixties. We need innovators and producers of positive change. The older generation's resistance to change is natural; so how do we change without alienating them? How can we reduce if not completely eliminate all the negativism, pettiness and cliquishness that exist and are so damaging? How can we enlarge the narrow choice factor—where in most cases our reality is controlled by Christianity, drugs, or alcohol? How can we create a common consciousness, based on a proven humanism—as we stop trying to prove our humanism to those who are unhuman? It's on us; nobody, nowhere will do it for us.

144

We Walk the Way of the New World. It's new. As indicated above, we are much louder, but softer, a logical progression, still screaming like a super-sonic wind tuned to a special frequency, but hip enough to realize that even some of those brothers and sisters tuned in will still not hear. The new book is in three parts: *Black Woman Poems, African Poems,* and *New World Poems.* Each part is a part of the other: Blackwoman is African and Africa is Blackwoman and they both represent the *New World.*

Actually all three sections are reflections of one blackman—which is to say that the whole book is based upon the direction I feel blackmen should be traveling. When we talk about nationalism, we mean *real* nationalism—that which embodies culture, politics, defense, and economy. We talk about a nationalism that will draw brothers and sisters into self and not alienate them; will answer questions and not only present problems; will build people, not individuals, with leadership qualities. That is, each one of us must possess those qualities of good leadership—a community of leaders —not just followers—who can and will work together. Remember *a leader is not only one that leads but is the best example of that leadership.*

Blackman/ an unfinished history

the old musicman   beat into an alien image of nothingness
we
remember you & will not forget
the days, the nights, the weekends
the secret savings for the trip north
or up south. We entered the new cities—
they were not ready for us—
those on the great rivers, the lakes

145

they were clean then, somewhat pure,
u cd even drink fr/ them
& the fish lived there in abundance.
we came by backseat greyhound & special trains
up south came us
to become a part of the pot that was supposed to melt
                    it did and we burned
and we burned into something different & unknown
we acquired a new ethic   a new morality   a new history
and we lost
we lost much   we lost that   that was
we became americans   the best   the real
and blindly adopted america's heroes as our own
our minds wouldn't *function.*
what was wrong?
it couldn't have been the air   it was clean then.

today
from the clouds we look back
seat 16C in the bird with the golden wings.
we came & were different shades of darkness
& we brought our music & dance,
that which wasn't polluted.
we took on the language, manners, mores, dress & religion
of the people with the unusual color.
into the 20th century we wandered rubber-stamped
a poor copy!

but the music was ours, the dance was ours, was ours.
& then it was hip—it was hip
to walk, talk & act a certain neighborhoodway,
we wore 24 hr sunglasses & called our woman *baby,*
our woman,
we wished her something else,

146

& she became that wish.
she developed into what we wanted,
she not only reflected *her,* but reflected us,
was a mirror of our death-desires.
we failed to protect or respect her
& no one else would,
& we didn't understand, we didn't understand.
why,
she be doing the things she don't do.

the sixties brought us black
at different levels, at different colors we searched
while   some of us still pissed into the wind.
we tasted
& turned our heads into a greater vision.
greatness becomes our new values—OOOOOOOO
like   telling yr daughter she's beautiful
& meaning *it.* Vee. Boom   Veeeee   Boom
You going to do it jim! BOOOOOOOOM
You goin ta jump around & startle the world blackman.
goin ta space man, all u got ta do is think space thoughts.
You're *slick* jim, yes you is
slicker than a oil slick, yes you is
just been sliding in the wrong direction. click.
be a *New World* picture.   click,   click.
blackman click blackman click into tomorrow.
Spaced from the old thoughts into
the new. Zooomm. Zoooommmmm   Zooommmmmm.
click.
design yr own neighborhoods,   Zoom   it can be,
teach yr own children,   Zoom   Zoom   it can be,
build yr own loop,   Zoom   Zoom   it can be,
feed yr own people.   Zoom   Zoom   it can be,

147

Watch out world greatness is coming.   click   click.
protect yr own communities,   Zoom   Zoom   it can be.

create *man* blackman. . . .
walk thru the
world
as if You are world itself,   click.
be an extension of everything beautiful & powerful,   click
click.
HEY   blackman look like
you'd be named something
like . . . . *earth, sun*
or *mountain.*
Go head, *universe*
Zoommmmmmmm.   Zooommmmmmmmm
Zoooommmmmmmmmmmmmm   click   click.
be it,
blackman.

As-Salaam-Alaikum,
Don L. Lee

BLACKWOMAN POEMS

soft: the way her eyes view her children.
hard: her hands; a comment on her will.
warm: just the way she is, jim!
sure: as yesterday, she's tomorrow's tomorrow.

Naked woman, black woman

Clothed with your colour which is life, with your form which is beauty!

In your shadow I have grown up; the gentleness of your hands was laid over my eyes.

And now, high up on the sun-baked pass, at the heart of summer, at the heart of noon, I come upon you, my Promised land,

And your beauty strikes me to the heart like the flash of an eagle.

—Leopold Sedar Senghor

Judy-One

she's the camera's
subject:
the sun for colored film.

her smile is like
clear light bouncing off
the darkness of the
mediterranean at nighttime.

we all know it,
her smile.
when it's working,
moves like sea water—
always going somewhere

strongly.

Man Thinking About Woman

some thing is lost in me,
like
the way you lose old thoughts   that
somehow seemed unlost at the right time.

i've not known it or you many days;
we met as friends with an absence of strangeness.
it was the month
that my lines got longer & my metaphors softer.

it was the week   that
i felt the city's narrow breezes rush about
me
looking for a place to disappear
as   i walked the clearway,
sure footed in used sandals screaming to be replaced

your empty shoes (except for used stockings)
partially hidden beneath the dresser
looked at me,
as i sat thoughtlessly   waiting
for your touch.

that day,
as your body rested upon my chest
i saw the shadow of the
window blinds   beam
across the unpainted ceiling
going somewhere
like the somewhere i was going
when
the clearness of yr/ teeth,
& the scars on yr/ legs stopped me.

your beauty: un-noticed by regular eyes   is
like   a blackbird resting
on a telephone wire   that moves
quietly with the wind.

a southwind.

Marlayna

harlem's night upon the world
women there
are drops of algerian sand
with joyeyes overworked to welcome.
beauty flows the curves of her natural,
hangs
on out like saturday night skipping sunday
she walks/moves the natureway.
to a hungry man
she's his watermelon.

154

Big Momma

finally retired   pensionless
from cleaning somebody else's house
she remained home to clean
the one she didn't own.

in her kitchen where we often talked
the *chicago tribune* served as a tablecloth
for the two cups of tomato soup that went
along with my weekly visit & talkingto.

she was in a seriously-funny mood
& from the get-go she was down, realdown:

>> roaches around here are like
>> letters on a newspaper
>> or
>> u gonta be a writer, hunh
>> when u gone write me some writen
>> or
>> the way niggers act around here
>> if talk cd kill we'd all be dead.

she's somewhat confused about all this *blackness*
but said that it's good when negroes start putting themselves
first and added: we've always shopped at the colored stores,
>> & the way niggers cut each other up round
>> here every weekend that whiteman don't
>>> haveta

worry bout no revolution specially when he's
gonta haveta pay for it too, anyhow all he's
  gotta do is drop a truck load of *dope* out
    there
on 43rd st. & all the niggers & yr
  revolutionaries
be too busy getten high & then they'll turn
  round
and fight each other over who got the
  mostest.

we finished our soup and i moved to excuse myself,
as we walked to the front door she made a last comment:
          now *luther* i knows you done changed a lots but if
          you can think back, we never did eat too much pork
          round here anyways, it was bad for the belly.
i shared her smile and agreed.

touching the snow lightly i headed for 43rd st.
at the corner i saw a brother crying   while
trying to hold up a lamp post,
thru his watery eyes i cd see big momma's words.

at sixty-eight
she moves freely, is often right
and when there is food
eats   joyously with her own
real teeth.

Mixed Sketches

u feel that way sometimes
wondering:
as a nine year old sister
with burned out hair oddly
smiles at you and sweetly calls you
brother.

u feel that way sometimes
wondering:
as a blackwoman & her 6 children
are burned out of their apartment with no place
to go & a nappy-headed nigger comes running thru
our neighborhood with a match in his hand cryin
revolution.

u feel that way sometimes
wondering:
seeing sisters in two hundred dollar wigs & suits
fastmoving in black clubs in late surroundings   talking
about late thoughts in late language waiting for late men
that come in with, "i don't want to hear bout nothing black
    tonight."

u feel that way sometimes
wondering:
while eating on newspaper tablecloths
& sleeping on clean bed sheets that couldn't
stop bed bugs   as black children watch their
mothers leave the special buses returning from
special neighborhoods
to clean their "own" unspecial homes.

u feel that way sometimes
wondering:
wondering, how did we survive?

Man and Woman
(for earnie, 1964)

two baths in one day!
at first i thought that you
just wanted to be clean.
then, u pulled the lights off
& the darkness took me away from my book.
lightly,
i asked about your perfume
u answered,
& added that u splashed it in unknown & strange places
and again lightly,
i asked,
if the perfume was *black.*
at first
our backs touched & we both played sleep.
u turned toward me
& the warmth of yr/blood rushes over me   as
u throw yr/left leg over my left leg
& get dangerous, very dangerous with yr/left hand.
the soul-station comes on automatically
with the aid of yr/right hand.
ike & tina turner are singing "get back"
from yr/touch i flinch and say,
listen to the record, woman!
you don't and i don't   while
"get back" is in rhythm
with the shaking of the bed
that's
mixed with our soft voices
that undoubtedly are heard unconfused through
thin walls.

Blackgirl Learning

she couldn't quote french poetry
that doesn't mean that she ain't read any
probably not
tho gwendolyn brooks & margaret walker
lined her dresser.

she did tell me that
the bible was pure literature
& she showed me her own poetry.
far beyond love verse (& it didn't rhyme)
she wrote about her man.

she said that her man
worshiped her,
he wasn't there.
she told me that he had other things to do:

learning to walk straight.

159

After her Man had left her
for the Sixth time that year
(an uncommon occurrence)

> she stood nakedly,
> nakedly
> against the window's cool
>   (it feltgood)
> she and her shadow
> competing for the same color.
>
> she is what we wd call
> 4 foxes, god's gift,
> a summer's dream: fall, winter & spring too.
> her silent movement brushed the window's cool.
>
> with a smile on her face
> she scoped his picture on the end-table
> (the only thing he didn't take)
>
> awkwardly,
> she stood nakedly,
> nakedly
> against the window's cool
> then
> joined it.

On Seeing Diana go Maddddddddd
(on the very special occasion of the death of her two dogs—
Tiffany & Li'l Bit—when she cried her eyelashes off)

a dog lover,
a lover of dogs   in a land where poodles
eat/live cleaner than their masters
& their masters use the colored people
to walk that   which they love, while they
wander in & out of our lives running the world.

(stop! in the name of love, before you break my heart)

u moved with childlike vision
deeper into lassieland to become
the new wonderwoman of the dirty-world
we remember the 3/ the three young baaaaad detroiters
of younger years when i & other blacks moved with u
& all our thoughts dwelled on the limits of forget & forgive.

(stop! in the name of love, before you break my heart)

diana,
we left u (back in those un-thinking days)   there
on the dance floor teaching marlon brando the monkey
(the only dance you performed with authority)
we washed our faces anew
as the two of you dreamed a single mind.
diana,
yr/ new vision worries me because i,
as once you, knew/know the hungry days   when

our fathers went to ford motor co.,
and our mothers
in the morning traffic to the residential sections of dearborn.
little surpreme, only the well fed *forget.*

(stop! in the name of love, before you break . . . . .)

ladies & gents we proudly present
the swinging sur-premessssss . . . . correction, correction.
ladies & gents we proudly present
diana rossss and the surpremes.
and there u stood,
a skinny earthling viewing herself as a mov
ing star. as a mov   ing star u will travel
north by northwest deeper into the ugliness
of yr/bent ego.   & for this i/we cannot forgive.

(stop! in the name of love, ...)

u, the gifted voice, a symphony, have now joined the
hippy generation to become unhipped,
to become the symbol of a new aberration,
the wearer of other people's hair.
to become one of the real animals of this earth.
we wish u luck & luckily u'll need it
in yr/new found image of a mov
ing star, a mov   ing star, mov   ing moving
moving on to play
a tooth-pick in a *rin tin tin* mov   ie.

first.
a woman should be
a woman first,
if she's anything.
but
if she's black, *really* black
and a woman
that's special, that's
realspecial.

AFRICAN POEMS

WE'RE an Africanpeople
hard-softness burning black.
the earth's magic color our veins.
an Africanpeople are we;
burning blacker softly, softer.

We the vomit of slavers
we the venery of the Calebars
what? that we should stuff our ears?
We, made dead drunk with the ship's rolling,
with jeers, with the sea-fog inhaled!
Forgive us, whirlpool our accomplice!

—*Aimé Césaire*

When I speak of the African genius, I mean something
different from negritude, something not apologetical, but
dynamic.

I do not mean a vague brotherhood based on a criterion of
colour, or on the idea that Africans have no reasoning but
only a sensitivity. By the African genius I mean something
positive, our socialist conception of society, the efficiency and
validity of our traditional statecraft, our highly developed
code of morals, our hospitality and our purposeful energy.

—*Kwame Nkrumah*

166

A Poem for A Poet
(for brother Mahmood Darweesh)

read yr/exile
i had a mother too,
& her death will not be
talked of around the world.
like you,
i live/walk a strange land.
my smiles are real but seldom.

our enemies eat the same bread
and their waste
(there is always waste)
is given to the pigs,
and then they consume the pigs.

Africa still has sun & moon,
has clean grass & water u can see thru;
Africa's people talk to u with their whole faces,
and their speech comes like drumbeats, comes like drumbeats.

our enemies eat the same bread
and the waste from their greed
will darken your sun and hide your moon,
will dirty your grass and mis-use your water.
your people will talk with unchanging eyes
and their speech will be slow & unsure & overquick.

Africa, be yr/own letters
or
all your people will want cars
and there are few roads.
you must eat yr/own food
and that which is left,
continue to share in earnest.

Keep your realmen; yr/sculptors
yr/poets, yr/fathers, yr/musicians, yr/sons, yr/warriors.
Keep your truemen of the darkskin,
a father guides his children,
keep them & they'll return your wisdom,
and
if you must send them,   send them
the way of the Sun
as to make them

blacker.

Change is Not Always Progress
(for Africa & Africans)

Africa.

don't let them
steal
your face   or
take your circles
and make them squares.

don't let them
steel
your body   as to put
100 stories of concrete on you
so that you
                 arrogantly
scrape
the

sky.

Knocking Donkey Fleas off a
Poet from the Southside of Chi
(for brother ted joans)

a worldman.
with the careful eye; the deep look, the newest look.
as recent & hip as the uncola being sipped by
thelonious monk
jackie-ing it down to little *rootie tootie's.*

he's a continent jumper,
a show-upper, a neo-be-bopper.
he's the first u see the last to flee,
the homeboy in African land;
with an inner compass of the rightway.
at times he's the overlooked   like
a rhinoceros in a bird bath.

the sound of his trumpet is the true *off minor.*
to hear him tell it: *bird* is alive, blacks must colonize europe,
                jazz is a woman & I did, I was, I am.
& I believe him.

170

he's younger than his poems
& old as his clothes,
he's badder than bad: him so bad he cd take a banana from a
                          gorilla, pull a pork chop out of a lion's
                          buttocks   or debate the horrors of
                          war with spiro agnew with his mouth
                          closed.
a worldman,
a man of his world.

ted joans is the tan of the sun; the sun's tan.
a violent/ peace
looking for a piece.
he'll find it   (in the only place he hasn't been)

among the stars,   that star.
the one that's missing.
last seen
walking slowly across Africa
bringing the rest of the world with it.

NEW WORLD POEMS

change.
create a climate for
change.
yesterday's weather has been un-
changeable.
there is a young dark storm coming;
has   nappy-hair.

The Negro rebellion marks the coming to power of activists who are disenchanted with both the white and black power elites . . . Like all social upheavals, the Negro rebellion is not one but two revolutions—a revolution against the militant-moderate within and the reactionary without . . . .

the growth of the Negro middle class which had the foresight and ingenuity to give birth to *radical* children. . . .

—*Lerone Bennett, Jr.*

My people, black and black, revile the River.
Say that the River turns, and turn the River.

—*Gwendolyn Brooks*

Our culture revolution must be the means of bringing us closer to our African brothers and sisters. It must begin in the community and be based on community participation. Afro-Americans will be free to create only when they can depend on the Afro-American community for support, and the Afro-American artists must realize that they depend on the Afro-American community for inspiration.

—*Al Hajj Malik al Shabazz*

Sun House
(a living legend)

        his fingers leaned
        forcefully against the neck
        of a broken gin bottle
        that
        rubbed gently on
        the steel strings of a borrowed guitar.

        the roughness of his voice
        is only matched by his immediate
        presence that is lifted into
        life with lonely words: "is u is or is u ain't
                    my baby, i say,
                    is u is or is u ain't
                    my baby, if u ain't
                    don't confess it now."

        to himself he knew the answers
        & the answers were amplified
        by the sharpness of the broken bottle
        that gave accent
        to the muddy music as it screamed
        & scratched the unpure lines
        of our many faces,
        while our bodies jumped to the sounds of

        mississippi.

One Sided Shoot-out
(for brothers fred hampton & mark clark, murdered
12/4/69 by chicago police at 4:30 AM while they slept)

only a few will really understand:
it won't be yr/mommas or yr/brothers & sisters or even me,
we all think that we do   but we don't.
it's not *new*   and
under all the rhetoric the seriousness is still not serious.
the national rap deliberately continues, "wipe them niggers
     out."
(no talk do it, no talk do it, no talk do it, notalk notalknotalk
     do it)

& we.
running circleround getting caught in our own cobwebs,
in the same old clothes, same old words, just new adjectives.
we will order new buttons & posters with: "remember fred"
     & "rite-on mark."
& yr/pictures will be beautiful & manly with the deeplook/
     the accusing look
to remind us
to remind us that suicide is not black.

the questions will be asked & the answers will be the new
     cliches.
but maybe,
just maybe we'll finally realize that "revolution" to the real-
     world
is international 24hours a day and that 4:30AM is like
     12:00 noon,
it's just darker.
but the evil can be seen if u look in the right direction.

176

were the street lights out?
did they darken their faces in combat?
did they remove their shoes to *creep* softer?
could u not see the whi-te of their eyes,
the whi-te of their deathfaces?
didn't yr/look-out man see them coming, coming, coming?
or did they turn into ghostdust and join the night's fog?

it was mean.
& we continue to call them "pigs" and "muthafuckas"
        forgetting what all
black children learn very early: "sticks & stones may break
                          my bones but names can
                          never hurt me."
it was murder.
& we meet to hear the speeches/ the same, the duplicators.
they say that which is expected of them.
to be instructive or constructive is to be unpopular (like: the
        leaders only
sleep when there is a watchingeye)
but they say the right things at the right time, it's like a
    stageshow:
only the entertainers have changed.
we remember bobby hutton.   the same,   the duplicators.

the seeing eye should always see.
the night doesn't stop the stars
& our enemies scope the ways of blackness in three bad shifts
        a day.
in the AM their music becomes deadlier.
this is a game of dirt.

only blackpeople play it **fair.**

FOR BLACK PEOPLE

(& negroes too. a poetic statement on black existence in
america with a view of tomorrow. all action takes place on
the continent of north america. these words, imperfect as they
may be, are from positive images received from gwendolyn
brooks, hoyt w. fuller, imamu baraka & joe goncalves.)

I: IN THE BEGINNING

state street was dead, wiped out.
ghetto expressways were up-lifted
and dropped on catholic churches.
all around us trees were being up rooted.
and flung into the entrances of bars, taverns & houses
of prostitution
lake meadows and prairie shores
passed our faces with human bodies of
black & whi-te mixed together, like salt & pepper,
—in concrete silence.
though deceased, some of the bodies still had smiles
—on their faces.
BONG BONG BONG BONG BONG BONG BONG
    BONG
IT STARTED LAST SUNDAY.
for some unknown reason all the baptist ministers—
    told the truth.
it was like committing mass suicide.
it was cold, mid-december, but the streets were hot.
the upward bound programs had failed that year.
the big bombs had been dropped, harlem &
    newark were annihilated.
another six million had perished and now
the two big men were fighting for universal survival.

178

the scene was blow for blow at the corner of 59th & racine,
right in front of the "Lead Me By the Hand"
    storefront church.
J.C., the blue eyed blond, had the upper hand for his
opponent, Allah, was weakening because of the strange—
    climate.
ahhhhh, ohoooooo, ahhaaaaa, ahhhaaaeeEEEE
in a bedroom across the street a blk/woman tearlessly
cries as she spread her legs, in hatred, for her landlord—
    paul goldstein.
(her children will eat tonight)
her brothers, boy-men called negroes, were off hiding
in some known place biting their nails & dreaming of
    whi-te virgins.
that year negroes continued to follow blind men whose
    eye-vision was less than their own & each morning
    negroes woke up a little deader.
the sun was less than bright, air pollution acted as a filter.
colored people were fighting each other knowingly
and little niggers were killing little niggers.
the "best" jobs were taken by colored college graduates
who had earned their degrees in a four year course of
    self-hatred with a minor in speech.
negroes religiously followed a blondhairedblueeyedman
    and no one forced them
whi-te boys continued to laugh and take blk/women.
negroes were unable to smile & their tears were dry. They
    had no eye-balls.
their sisters went to strangers' beds cursing them.
that year negroes read styron, mailer, joyce and rimbaud.
last year it was bellow, wallace, sartre & voznesensky
(yevtushenko was unpoetic).
somebody said that there was no such thing as black lit-

179

erature & anyway we all knew that negroes didn't write,
except occasional letters to the editor.
niggers 3 steps from being shoeshine boys were dressing
and talking like william buckley jr.—minus the pencil.
their heroes danced unclothed out of greek mythology.
janis smyth & claude iforgethislastname often quoted pas-
        sages from antigone (pronounced anti-gone).
the pope, all perfumed down—smelling like a french sissy,
watched 59th and racine from st. peters with a rosary
        in his hand:
                        hell mary full of grace the lord is with thee.
                        hell mary full of grace the lord is with thee.
                        hell mary full of grace the lord was with thee.
blk/poets were not citizens & were being imprisoned and
        put to death.
whi-te boys remained our teachers & taught the people
        of color
how to be negroes and homosexuals.
some invisible fiction writer continued to praise the pov-
        erty program & is now being considered for "negro
        writer in residence" at johnson city, texas.
a blind negro poet compared himself with yeats
not knowing that he, himself, was a "savage side show."
all this happened in the beginning
and the beginning is almost the end.

II. TRANSITION AND MIDDLE PASSAGE

gas masks were worn as were side-arms.
the two nations indivisible & black people began to believe
        in themselves.
muhammad ali remained the third world's champ &
        taught the people self defense.

blk/poets were released from prison & acted as consult-
    ants to the blk/nation.
there were regular napalm raids over the whi-te house.
college trained negroes finally realized that they weren't
    educated and expressed sorrow for losing their virginity
    in europe.
the urban progress centers were transformed into hospitals
    & the records were used for toilet paper.
the room was whi-te & the blacks entered only to find
    that the two colors wouldn't mix.
deee-bop a bop bop, dee dee abop, bop-o-bop dee dee,
    wee, WEEEEEE.
willie johnson, all processed down, was noticeably driving
down cottage grove in a gold & black deuce & a quarter;
hitting the steering wheel at 60 degrees off center, with
his head almost touching the right window. willie, dressed
in a gold ban-lon that matched his ride, slowly moved his
left foot to his dual stereo that coolly gave out jerry
butler's: "never gone ta give you up."
while miss wilberforce, alias miss perm of 1967, tried
to pass him on his right side in her pine-yellow 287 must-
ang with the gas tank always on full. dressed in a two
piece beige marshall field's o-ri-ginal, miss perm with hair
flowing in the wind was nodding her head to the same
tune:
        "never gone ta give you up."
both, the stang & the deuce hit the corner of 39th & cottage
at the same time; and as if somebody said, "black is
beautiful," miss perm and processed-down looked at each
other with educated eyes that said:
                        i hate you.
that year even lovers didn't love.
whi-te boys continued to take blk/women to bed; but they

ceased to wake up alive.
this was the same year that the picture "Guess Who's
    Coming to Dinner" killed spencer tracy.
negro pimps were perpetual victims of assassination &
    nobody cried.
Amiri Baraka wrote the words to the blk/national anthem &
    pharoah sanders composed the music. tauhid became
    our war song.
an alive wise man will speak to us, he will quote du bois,
nkrumah, coltrane, fanon, muhammad, trotter and him-
    self. we will listen.
chicago became known as negro-butcher to the world &
    no one believed it would happen, except the jews—the
    ones who helped plan it.
forgetting their own past—they were americans now.
eartha kitt talked to nbc about blk/survival; receiving
    her instructions from the bedroom at night.
blk/people stopped viewing TV & received the new
    messages from the talking drum.
dope pushers were given over doses of their own junk
    & they died. no one cried.
united fruit co. & standard oil were wiped out & whi-te
    people cried.
at last, the president could not control our dreams
and the only weapon he could threaten us with
    was death.

III. THE END IS THE REAL WORLD

it is a new day and the sun is not dead.
Allah won the fight at 59th & racine and his sons are not
    dead.
blk/poets are playing & we can hear. marvin x & Askia

182

Muhammad Touré walk the streets with smiles on their
faces. i join them. we talk & listen to our own words.
we set aside one day a year in remembrance of whi-tness.
                    (anglo-saxon american history day)
the air is clean. men & women are able to love.
legal holidays still fall in february: the 14th and 23rd*.
all the pigs were put to death, the ones with men-like
      minds too.
men stopped eating each other and hunger existed only in
      history books.
money was abolished and everybody was rich.
every home became a house of worship & pure water runs
      again.
young blk/poets take direction from older blk/poets &
      everybody listens.
those who speak have something to say & people seldom
      talk about themselves.
those who have something to say wait their turn & listen to
      their own message.
the hip thing is not to be cool & get high but to be cool &
      help yr/brother.
the pope retired & returned the land & valuables his
      organization had stolen under the guise of religion.
Allah became a part of the people & the people knew &
      loved him as they knew and loved themselves.
the world was quiet and gentle and beauty came back.
people were able to breathe.
blk/women were respected and protected & their actions
proved deserving of such respect & protection.
each home had a library that was overused.
the blackman had survived.

———
*Birth dates of Frederick Douglass and W. E. Du Bois

he was truly the "desert people."
there were black communities, red communities, yellow
    communities and a few whi-te communities that were
    closely watched.
there was not a need for gun control.
there was no need for the word peace for its
    antonym had been removed from the vocabulary.
like i sd befo
the end is the real world.

July, 1968

A Loneliness

looking thru the commercial
glass of the holidays or howard j's
(i failed to make a distinction)
after a long day at luther college, the one in iowa.
listening to the unimpressive
trying to impress.

i stood there
watching myself   feel
feeling
my own eyes   checking
my dark reflection against
the day's sounds.

standing there   listening
as the rain drops dropped
over the dead leaves
that
rested on the greenless grass
as the tree's shadow
played dodge   with the slow wind.

at night the distant
street light is the brightest sun
and i go to bed
feeling
a part of it.

See Sammy Run in the Wrong Direction
(for the ten *negro* editors representing n.n.p.a. who
visited occupied *Palestine* [known as Israel] on a fact finding
trip, but upon their return—reported few facts, if any.)

we know others.
are u others, or are u inbetweens?
imitation imitations. like junior sammy davises
kissing the wailing wall
in the forgotten occupied country.
his top lip stuck
& in a strange land he hollered for his momma
not being jewish
naturally
she was off some place   being herself.

with his bottom lip free
he talked to himself as his bad eye
saw the wall coming
even at the deathmoment he tried to steal
the newsong.
afterall
he was just a jewish boy
who happened to be negro.

186

the deathmoment coming, the wall.
& the jewishnegro tried his infamous impersonations:
                cagney, sullivan, bogart, martin,
                lewis, durante, lawford, sinatra,
                with tom jones & janis joplin both
                singing, "i wish i was black."

but the good eye saw
the realdeath   the certaindeath
while the brainmessages charged the body
for the impression of impressions
& sammy tried but his blood was   gone
                        his inner self was   gone
                        his hair turned   back
and
he began to really see
as the wall came,
it failed and   he failed   to do
an impression of a

blackman.

We Walk the Way of the New World

1.

we run the dangercourse.
the way of the stocking caps & murray's grease.
(if u is modern u used duke greaseless hair pomade)
jo jo was modern/ an international nigger
                born: jan. 1, 1863 in new york, mississippi.
his momma was mo militant than he was/ is
jo jo bes no instant negro
his development took all of 106 years
& he was the first to be stamped "made in USA"
where he arrived bow-legged a curve ahead of the 20th
        century's new weapon: television.
which invented, "how to win and influence people"
& gave jo jo his how/ ever look: however u want me.

we discovered that with the right brand of cigarettes
that one, with his best girl,
cd skip thru grassy fields in living color
& in slow-motion: Caution: niggers, cigarette smoking
                will kill u & yr/ health.
& that the breakfast of champions is: blackeyed peas & rice.
& that God is dead & Jesus is black and last seen on 63rd
            street in a gold & black dashiki, sitting in a pink
            hog speaking swahili with a pig-latin accent.
& that integration and coalition are synonymous,
& that the only thing that really mattered was:
        who could get the highest on the least or how to expand
        & break one's mind.

in the coming world
new prizes are
to be given

we *ran* the dangercourse.
now, it's a silent walk/ a careful eye
jo jo is there
to his mother he is unknown
(she accepted with a newlook: what wd u do if someone
     loved u?)
jo jo is back
& he will catch all the new jo jo's as they wander in & out
and with a fan-like whisper say: you ain't no
                              tourist
                              and Harlem ain't for
                              sight-seeing, brother.

2.

Start with the itch and there will be no scratch. Study
    yourself.
Watch yr/ every movement as u skip thru-out the southside of
    chicago.
be hip to yr/ actions.

our dreams are realities
traveling the nature-way.
we meet them
at the apex of their utmost
meanings/ means;
we walk in cleanliness
down state st/ or Fifth Ave.
& wicked apartment buildings shake
as their windows announce our presence
as we jump into the interior
& cut the day's evil away.

We walk in cleanliness
the newness of it all
becomes us
our women listen to us
and learn.
We teach our children thru
our actions.

We'll become owners of the   New World
the New World.
will run it as unowners
for
we will live in it too
& will want to be remembered
as   realpeople.

190

Move Un-noticed to be Noticed:
A Nationhood Poem

move, into our own, not theirs
into our.
they own it (for the moment): the unclean world, the
polluted space, the un-censor-
ed air, yr/foot steps as they
run wildly in the wrong
direction.

move, into our own, not theirs
into our.
move, you can't buy own.
own is like yr/hair (if u let it live); a natural extension of
ownself.
own is yr/reflection, yr/total-being; the way u walk, talk,
dress and relate to each other is *own*.

own is you,
cannot be bought or sold: can u buy yr/writing hand
yr/dancing feet, yr/speech,
yr/woman (if she's real),
yr/manhood?

own is ours.
all we have to do is   *take it,*
take it the way u take from one another,
the way u take artur rubenstein over thelonious
monk,
the way u take eugene genovese over lerone bennett,
the way u take robert bly over imamu baraka,
the way u take picasso over charles white,
the way u take marianne moore over gwendolyn
brooks,
the way u take *inaction* over *action.*

move. move to act.   act.
act into thinking and think into action.
try to think. think.   try to think think think.
try to think. think (like i said, into yr/own) think.
try to think. don't hurt yourself, i know it's new.
try to act,
act into thinking and think into action.
can u do it, hunh? i say hunh, can u stop moving like a drunk
     gorilla?

                    ha ha   che che
                    ha ha   che che
                    ha ha   che che
                    ha ha   che che
move
what is u anyhow: a professional car watcher, a billboard for
     nothingness, a sane madman, a reincarnated clark gable?
either you is or you ain't!

the deadliving
are the worldmakers,
the image breakers,
the rule takers: blackman can you stop a hurricane?

"I remember back in 1954 or '55, in Chicago, when we had
13 days without a murder, that was before them colored
people started calling themselves *black*."
move.
move,
move to be moved,
move into yr/ownself, Clean.
Clean, u is the first black hippy i've ever met.
why u bes dressen so funny, anyhow, hunh?
i mean, is that u Clean?
why u bes dressen like an airplane, can u fly,

i mean,
will yr/ blue jim-shoes fly u,
& what about yr/ tailor made bell bottoms, Clean?
can they lift u above madness,
turn u into the right direction,
& that red & pink scarf around yr/ neck what's that for Clean,
hunh?   will it help u fly, yeah, swing, swing   ing swing
            swinging high above telephone wires with dreams
            of this & that and illusions of trying to take bar-b-q
            ice cream away from lion minded niggers who
            didn't even know that *polish* is more than a
            sausage.
"clean as a tack,
rusty as a nail,
haven't had a bath
sence columbus sail."

when u goin be something real, Clean?
like yr/ own, yeah, when u goin be yr/ ownself?

the deadliving
are the worldmakers,
the image breakers,
the rule takers: blackman can u stop a hurricane, mississippi
        couldn't.
blackman if u can't stop what mississippi couldn't, *be it. be it.*
blackman be the wind, be the win, the win, the win, win win:

            wooooooooooowe boom boom   wooooooooooowe bah
            wooooooooooowe boom boom   wooooooooooowe bah
if u can't stop a hurricane, be one.
            wooooooooooowe boom boom   wooooooooooowe bah
            wooooooooooowe boom boom   wooooooooooowe bah

be the baddddest hurricane that ever came, a black hurricane.

    woooooooooowe boom boom   wooooooooooowe bah

    woooooooooowe boom boom   wooooooooooowe bah

the badddest black hurricane that ever came, a black

        hurricane named Beulah,

go head Beulah, do the hurricane.

    wooocooooooowe boom boom   wooooooooooowe bah

    woooooooooowe boom boom   woooooooooowe bah

move

move to be moved from the un-moveable,

into our own, yr/self is own, yrself is own, own yourself.

go where you/we go, hear the unheard and do,

do the undone, do it, do it, do it *now,* Clean

and tomorrow your sons will

be alive to praise

you.

change-up,
let's go for ourselves
both cheeks are broken now.
change-up,
move past the corner bar,
let yr/ spirit lift u above that quick high.
change-up,
that tooth pick you're sucking on was
once a log.
change-up,
and yr/ children will look at u differently
than   we looked at our parents.

Directionscore

1970-1971

a smile at the right time
can be the most revolutionary act
that one can commit

"The cold fact is that whether or not a national literature gains international recognition has nothing to do with quality. It is all politics. If a country is a political power, its literature becomes recognized. This was shortly after the Middle East Six Day War, and the boom in Israeli and Yiddish literature was well on its way."

—*Joseph Okpaku*

Positives: for Sterling Plumpp

can u walk away from ugly,
will u sample the visions of yr self,
is ugly u? it ain't yr momma, yr woman,
> the brother who stepped on yr alligator shoes,
> yr wig wearen believen in Jesus grandmomma, or
> the honda ridden see-thru jump suit wearen brother.

yeah,
caught u upsidedown jay-walking across europe
to catch badness running against yr self.
didn't u know u were lost brother?
confused hair with blackness
thought u knew it before the knower did,
didn't u know u lost brother?
thought u were bad until u ran up against BAD:
Du Pont, Ford, General Motors   even the latest
Paris fashions: & u goin ta get rich off dashikis before Sears.
didn't u know u were lost brother?

beat laziness back into the outside,
run the mirror of ugliness into its inventors,
will u sample the visions of yr self?
quiet   like the way u do it soft spoken   quiet
quiet   more dangerous than danger a new   quiet
quiet   no name quiet no number quiet pure   quiet
quiet   to pure to purer.

a full-back clean-up man   a black earthmover
my main man
change yr name like the wind
blow in any direction catch righteousness,
u may have ta smile at the big preacher in town,
thats alright organize in the church washroom,

trick the brother into learning—
be as together as a 360 computer:
        can u think as well as u talk,
        can u read as well as u drink,
        can u teach as well as u dress?
sample the new visions of yr work brother   & smile
we'll push DuBois like they push the racing form.

yr woman goin ta look up to u,
yr children goin ta call u hero,
u my main nigger
the somethin like the somethin
u ain't suppose   *to be.*

With All Deliberate Speed
(for the children of our world)

in july of 19 somethin
the year of the "love it or leave it" stickers,
a pink sharecropper former KKK   now
a wallacite pro-bircher
undercover minuteman
living in N.Y. city   as
a used hardhat flag waving,
beer belly torn undershirt wearen
hawk.

is also
an unread bible carrying preacher
& secret draft dodger from WW 2
who
went to washington d.c.
at government's expense   for
the 1970 honor america day   and
support our boys in viet nam
also
took time out to find
& wildly   slap   slap   slap   slap
one
B.A., M.A., LLD., N.E.G.R.O.,
supreme court justice in the mouth   and
with all deliberate speed
went home to alabama
to brag about
it.

To be Quicker
for Black Political Prisoners
on the inside & outside—real
(to my brothers & sisters of OBAC)

clamb ape mountain backwards
better than the better u thought u had to be better than
jump clean.   cleaner.
jump past lightning into field-motion, feel-motion, feel mo
feel mo than the world thought u capable of feelin.
cd do it even fool yr momma, jim! fool yrself, hunh—

goin ta be cleaner,   hunh.
goin ta be stronger,   hunh.
goin ta be wiser,   hunh.
goin ta be quick to be quicker   *to be.*

quick to be whats needed to be   whats needed:
quicker than enemies of the livingworld,
quicker than cheap smiles of a cadillac salesman,
quicker than a dead junky talkin to the wind,
quicker than super-slick niggers sliding in the opposite,
quicker than whi-te-titty-new-left-what's-left suckin niggers,
quicker to be quick, to be quick.

u wise brother.
u wiser than my father was   when he
talked the talk   he wasn't suppose to talk.

quicker to be quick, to be:

a black-African-fist slapping a wop-dope pusher's momma,
a hospital a school anything workin to save us to pull us
closer to Tanzania to Guinea to Harlem to the West Indies to
closer to momma to sister to brother closer to closer to
FRELIMO to Rastafory to us to power to running run to build

to controllifelines to Ashanti to music to life to Allah closer
to Kenya to the black world to the rays of anti-evil.

clamb ape mountain backwards   brother
feel better than the better u thought was better
its yr walk brother,
lean a little, cut the smell of nasty.
jump forward into the past
to bring back

goodness.

An Afterword: for Gwen Brooks
(the search for the new-song begins with the old)

knowing her is not knowing her.

is not
autograph lines or souvenir signatures & shared smiles,
is not
pulitzers, poet laureates or honorary degrees
you see   we ordinary people
just know
ordinary people.

to read gwen is to be,
to experience her in the *real*
is the same, she is her words,   more
like a fixed part of the world   is there
quietly penetrating   slow
reminds us of a willie kgositsile love poem   or
issac hayes singing *one woman.*

still
she suggests more;
have u ever seen her home?
it's an idea of her: a brown wooden frame
trimmed in dark gray with a new screen door.
inside: looks like the lady owes everybody on the southside
            nothing but books momma's books.
her home like her person is under-fed and small.

204

gwen:
pours smiles of african-rain
a pleasure well received among uncollected garbage cans
and heatless basement apartments.
her voice the needle for new-songs
plays unsolicited messages: poets, we've all seen
poets. minor poets ruined by
minor fame.

Mwilu/or Poem for the Living
(for charles & Latanya)

jump bigness upward
like u jump clean   make everyday the weekend
& work like u party.

u justice brother, in the world of the un
just be there when wanted when needed when
yr woman calls yr name Musyoka* when yr son
wants direction strength give it, suh. suh
we call u strength suh, call u whatever.

be other than the common   build the sky
work;
study the bringers of anti-good,
question Jesus in the real,
& walk knowledge like you walk unowned streets, brother.
read like u eat   only betta   betta Musemi,*
Musemi be yr name   run emptiness into its givers
& collect the rays of wisdom.
there's goodness in yr eyes giver,   give.
yr wind is chicago-big, Kitheka: Afrikan forest right-wind
running waking dullness of the night-thinkers in the wrong.

why we rather be evil, momma?
why we ain't togatha, Rev. Cleopelius?
why we slide under with tight smiles of forgiveness, Judas?
why our women want to be men, Amana?
why our men want to be somethin other, Muthusi?
what's goin ta make us   us, Kimanthi?
why we don't control our school, Mr. Farmer?
why we don't have any land, big negro?
why we against love, pimps?

FRELIMO* in chicago talkin to the *stones*
hear what the real rocks have ta say.
be strange in the righteous
move away dumbjunkies leaning into death:

     never Muslim eating pig sandwiches   never
     never listerine breath even cuss proper   never
     never u ignorant because *smart* was yr teacher   never
     never wander under wonder fan-like avenues   never
     never *will be never* as long as never teaches   never.

snatching answers from the blue   while
giving lip-service   before imitating yr
executers.

jump bigness upward
Impressions puttin Fanon to music & sing like
black-rubbermen over smoked garbage cans with
music of a newer year among stolen nights in
basement corners meet u in the show, baby
just below the health food sign by sam's with
clean water over oiled fish as mini skirt sisters
wear peace symbols supporting the Israelis as
unfeeling as the *east india company.* wdn't dance
to the words of Garvey on Pill hill eatin cornbread
with a fork in a see-thru walking suit while running
the fields of crazy while teaching the whi-te boy
the hand-shake. would sell yr momma if somebody wd buy
    her
hunh.   roach-back challenge space after un-eaten spit.
goin ta still call u brother,
goin ta still call u sister too, hunh.
brother, sister
young lovers of current doo-wops
rake cleanliness brother:

& study un-written words of manhood.
young lovers of current doo-wops
what's yr new name sister:
reflect the goodness of yr man.
like the way u talk to each other,   like it.
the way yr voices pull smiles
u + u = 2 over 2 which is 1.

raised higher than surprised quietness
kiss each other   and
touch the feel of secret words
while we all walk the
shadows of greatness.

---

*The African names used are from the Swahili language of central & east Africa.
Mwilu (Mwi-lu)—of black; likes black
Musyoka (Mu-syo-ka)—one who always returns
Musomi (Mu-so-mi)—scholarly; reads; studies
Kitheka (Ki-*the*-ka)—wanderer of the forest
Amana (A-ma-na)—peacefulness; serenity; feminine
Kimanthi (Ki-ma-*nthi*)—one who searches for freedom, wealth, love
FRELIMO—Freedom fighters from Mozambique (south-east Africa)